r: ***Jakob van Hoddis*** (1914)
und Tinte, 49,9 x 41,6 cm

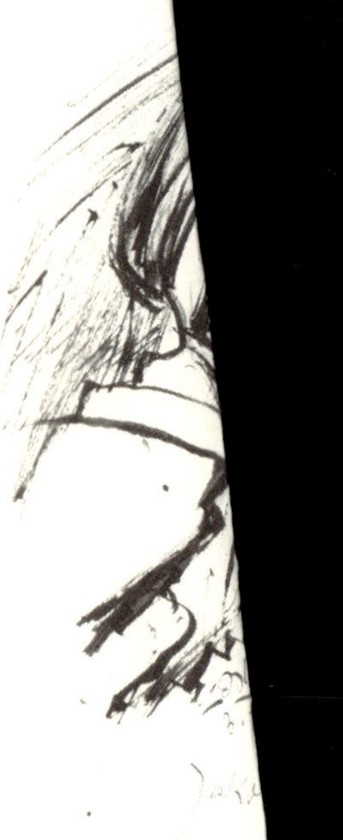

Ludwig Meidne
Bleistift, Pinsel

Jakob van Hoddis

Starker Wind über der bleichen Stadt

Strong Wind Over the Pale City

Gedichte / *Poems*

Herausgegeben von
Irene Stratenwerth

aus dem Deutschen übersetzt von
Mitch Cohen und Gregory Divers

PalmArtPress
Berlin

Dieser Band wurde durch die Ursula Lachnit-Fixson Stiftung, Berlin und die Erbengemeinschaft des Jakob van Hoddis/ Hans Davidsohn ermöglicht.

Bibliografische Information der Deutschen Nationalbibliothek
Die Deutsche Nationalbibliothek verzeichnet diese Publikation in der Deutschen Nationalbibliografie; detaillierte bibliografische Daten sind im Internet über http://www.d-nb.de abrufbar.

ISBN: 978-3-96258-033-9

PalmArtPress
Verlegerin: Catharine J. Nicely
Pfalzburgerstr. 69, 10719 Berlin
www.palmartpress.com

Umschlaggestaltung: Catharine J. Nicely
Druck u. Bindung: Opolgraf

Hergestellt in Europa

Inhalt / Content

Veröffentlichungen zu Lebzeiten
Publications in his Lifetime

Gedichte aus dem Nachlass
Poems from the Literary Estate

Tristitia ante …

Schneeflocken fallen. Meine Nächte sind
Sehr laut geworden, und zu starr ihr Leuchten.
Alle Gefahren, die mir ruhmvoll deuchten,
Sind nun so widrig wie der Winterwind.

Ich hasse fast die helle Brunst der Städte.

Wenn ich einst wachte und die Mitternächte
Langsam zerflammten – bis die Sonne kam –,
Wenn ich den Prunk der weißen Huren nahm,
Ob magrer Prunk mir endlich Lösung brächte,

War diese Grelle nie und dieser Gram.

Tristitia ante …

Snowflakes fall. My radiant nights' great din
Has grown so loud, and much too rigid to see.
All dangers that once seemed so glorious to me
Are now as woeful as the winter wind.

I almost hate the brightness of the cities' mating grunt.

When I held watch betimes, and every midnight
Slowly flamed away until the sun's return,
If never white whores' splendor did I spurn,
Whether slender splendor at last brought me respite,

Never was this glare and grief but half as grimly blunt.

Aurora

Nach Hause stiefeln wir verstört und alt,
Die grelle, gelbe Nacht hat abgeblüht.
Wir sehn, wie über den Laternen, kalt
Und dunkelblau, der Himmel droht und glüht.

Nun winden sich die langen Straßen, schwer
Und fleckig, bald, im breiten Glanz der Tage.
Die kräftige Aurore bringt ihn her,
Mit dicken rotgefrorenen Fingern, zage.

Aurora

Boots tromping homeward, we're troubled and old,
The glaring yellow bloom of night did fade and blow.
We see how, hovering above the lanterns, cold
And dark blue, the threatening heavens glow.

Now the long streets twist about, severe
And spotty in the vast, bright daytime sky.
Mighty Aurora beckons this grandeur here
With meaty, rosy-frozen fingers – shy.

Weltende

Dem Bürger fliegt vom spitzen Kopf der Hut,
In allen Lüften hallt es wie Geschrei.
Dachdecker stürzen ab und gehn entzwei
Und an den Küsten – liest man – steigt die Flut.

Der Sturm ist da, die wilden Meere hupfen
An Land, um dicke Dämme zu zerdrücken.
Die meisten Menschen haben einen Schnupfen.
Die Eisenbahnen fallen von den Brücken.

End of the World

From the burgher's pointy head, wind takes his hat.
All the air resounds with shrieks and cries.
Steeplejacks plunge from rooftops and so go splat.
And on the coasts – we read – the waters rise.

The storm has come; the wild seas hop and skip
Onto land; great dams are crushed by watery pestles.
Most people have post-nasal drip.
And trains are toppling from the trestles.

Varieté

I
Loge

Ein Walzer rumpelt, geile Geigen kreischen;
Die Luft ist weiß vom Dunst der Zigaretten;
Es riecht nach Moschus, Schminke, Wein, nach fetten
Indianern und entblößten Weiberfleischen.

Ah! schwimmen in der dicken Luft die vielen
Dämlichen Köpfe, die ins Helle glotzen?
Drei Weiber läßt man auf der Bühne spielen,
Die süßlich mit gemeinen Gesten protzen.

II
Der Athlet

Und der Athlet tritt auf und staunen kannste,
Wie er ein Brett mit seiner Faust zerhaut.
Er geht einher mit ungeheurem Wanste
Und feistem Arm und Nacken, schweißbetaut.

Und kurze Hosen schlottern um die Beinchen,
Die sind zu dünnen Stöckchen deformiert.
Prunkende Seide seine Füßchen ziert.
Ach! Sind die niedlich! Wie zwei rosa Schweinchen.

Vaudeville

I
Loge

A waltz ker-thumps; horny fiddles kvetch.
The air is white with smoke from cigarettes.
It reeks of musk and makeup, wine, of wretched
Fat Injuns and buck-naked female flesh.

Ah! Is the air near thick as clay,
So that stupid noggins swim and in the brightness stare?
Three broads are sent onto the stage to play
And cloyingly flaunt the crudest gestures they could dare.

II
The Strongman

The athlete enters and he's oohed
And aahed as fist meets board with a smash.
He struts his paunch with prodigious panache,
His bull-like arms and nape sweat-bedewed.

And short pants flutter 'round his legs –
Withered and deformed like spindly twiglets.
Sumptuous silk adorns his feet, the tiny pegs.
Awww! Ain't they cute! Like two pink piglets.

III
Der Humorist

Ein alter Mann in einem neuen Fracke
Plärrt nun seine Liebesabenteuer.
Und besonders nach gewissen neuern
Abenteuern,
Spricht er, gleiche er dem Wracke,
Das auf den Wellen wackle ohne Rast,
Der Winds-»Braut« preisgegeben, ohne Steuer,
Sogar mit halb verfaultem »Mast«.

IV
Tanz

Ein kleines Mädchen mit gebrannten Löckchen
In einem Hemd ganz himmelblau –
Die bloßen Beine trippeln ohne Söckchen.
Sie singt: »Ach, tu mir nichts zuleide!
Ach Du! Heut werd ich Deine Frau!«

Dann tanzt sie gierig und mit Chic
Zu einer holprigen Musik.
Und durch die Wirbel blauer Seide
Siehste den jungen Leib genau.

III
The Comedian

An old man in a brand new tux
Whines about his amorous adventures,
And especially after certain recent ones,
Real indecent ones,
He says he's a wreck – his line as he fishes for yucks –
His deck wobbling restless on the waves (real gut-wrenchers),
Rudderless and utterly abandoned to the "bridal" winds
In which his "mast", half-rotten, bends.

IV
Dance

A little girl with curling-iron locks
In a blouse all heaven blue –
Legs bare, she scampers around, no socks,
And sings, "Oh, don't do me harm. Oh you!
Be nice, and tonight I'll be your girl!"

She dances, so greedy and so chic
To music bumbling and weak.
Spellbound by the sky-blue silken whirl,
You ogle the nubile body of this little girl.

V
Die Inderin

Sie hebt den dünnen Arm; da duckt zum Sprunge
Das dunkle Pantherpaar, durch sieben Reifen
Fährt es hindurch mit elegantem Schwunge.

Und ihre bösen starken Pranken streifen
(Wenn sie verwirrt zurück zum Käfig taumeln)
Die Perlenschnüre, die .. von einem lila Gurte ..
Um ihrer nackten Herrin Hüften baumeln.

VI
Ballet

Neger schlenkern aufrecht mit den Beinen,
Auf dem Rumpfe gelbliche Trikots.
Und dazwischen tanzen unsere frechen kleinen
Weiber blond und nackend; ganz famos
Angezogen:
Nur mit goldenen Stöckelschuhn,
Mit denen sie die fauchenden Athleten
Behende in die dicken Nasen treten.

V
The Woman from India

She lifts a slender arm. The panther pair
Crouches for the leap. Through seven hoops
They spring with elegance and flair.

As, dazed, they stagger to the cage (at center stage),
Their mighty claws and gleaming savage fangs
Brush a dangling string of pearls .. that hangs ..
From a lilac sash around their mistress' bare derriere.

VI
Ballet

Black men swing their legs, erect;
A yellow jersey every chest conceals.
Between them prance our sassy lassies, bedecked
So smashingly in naught but golden fuck-me heels
With which they, blonde and agile, strike their poses
And kick the snarling athletes' flat, wide noses.

VII
Die Soubrette

Ein Weibsbild kommt als Jägersmann
Und schießt auf ihrer Flinten.
Und sieht sich einen Vogel an
Und zeigt sich uns von hinten.

Ihr Hintern biegt sich unerhört
Auf Beinen stramm wie Säulen.
Sie singt: »Mich hat die Lieb verstört
Juchhei! im grünen Walde …«

VIII
Die Tänzerin

Wie mich die zärtlichen Gelenke rühren,
Dein magrer Nacken, Deiner Kniee Biegen!
Ich zürne fast. Werde ich Dir erliegen?
Wirst Du zu jenem Traum zurück mich führen,

Den ich als Knabe liebend mir erbaute
Aus süßen Versen und dem Spiel der schönen
Schauspielerinnen, linden Geigentönen
Und Idealen, die ich klaute?

Ach, keine fand ich jenem Traume gleich,
Ich mußte weinend Weib um Weib vermeiden.
Ich war verbannt zu unermessnem Leiden
Und hasse jenen Traum. Ich spähe bleich,

VII
The Soubrette

A dame appears, as huntsman dressed,
And fires off her gun.
Upon a bird her gaze alights to rest;
She shows her back to everyone.

Outrageously she bends her rear
On legs like pillars in a colonnade.
She sings, "Oh, love has left me sad and drear.
Holdari! Here in the greenwood glade!"

VIII
The Dancer

How your delicate limbs set my eyes a-gleam!
Your slender neck, the tender hollows of your knees!
I almost rage! By your charms I'm seized!
You lead me back to that beautiful dream

I'd so lovingly built as a boy
From the sweet poetry and beauty I found
In actresses' play, in soothing violin sound,
And in the stolen ideals of my joy.

That dream went unmatched in an endless chain
Of women I had to reject. And so I weep,
Exiled as I am in my measureless pain,
And hate every dream. Pale, I peep,

Und sorgsam späh ich, wie Dein Leib sich wende,
Nach jeder Fehle, die im Tanz Du zeigst,
Ich bin Dir dankbar, da Du doch am Ende
Mit einem blöden Lächeln Dich verneigst.

IX
Lebendes Bild

Zwei Skribenten mit zu großer Neese
Sitzen vor der Wand aus gelbem Taft;
Und sie sorgen sich um die Synthese
Der Kultur und um die Jungfernschaft.

Denn der Teufel schreitet durch die Mitte
Und ist gänzlich ohne innern Halt.
Feurig federn seine langen Schritte,
Schwarz und wechselnd ist er von Gestalt.

Und er wedelt mit dem schlangenhaften Schweife;
Denn er hat mit einer Maus gehurt,
Und im Vordergrund raucht schon die Pfeife
Seine neugeborne Mißgeburt.

Attentive to see your body contend
With every misstep and botched pirouette.
I'm grateful to you and relieved at the end, when
You curtsy and smile like a silly coquette.

IX
Tableau

Two scribes with shnozzes worth a prize
Sit before a wall of yellow tulle
And worry how to synthesize
Culture and virginity. They mull.

Through the middle strides the devil
Lacking any trace of inner stability.
His springy step's long, but not on the level;
He's black; his form? Mutability.

He waggles his snakelike tail,
For he went whoring with a snipe.
His newborn freak of nature seems quite hale,
And, in the foreground, puffs a pipe.

X
Schluß: Kinematograph

Der Saal wird dunkel. Und wir sehn die Schnellen
Der Ganga, Palmen, Tempel auch des Brahma,
Ein lautlos tobendes Familiendrama
Mit Lebemännern dann und Maskenbällen.

Man zückt Revolver, Eifersucht wird rege,
Herr Piefke duelliert sich ohne Kopf.
Dann zeigt man uns mit Kiepe und mit Kropf
Die Älplerin auf mächtig steilem Wege.

Es zieht ihr Pfad sich bald durch Lärchenwälder,
Bald krümmt er sich und dräuend steigt die schiefe
Felswand empor. Die Aussicht in der Tiefe
Beleben Kühe und Kartoffelfelder.

Und in den dunklen Raum – mir ins Gesicht –
Flirrt das hinein, entsetzlich! nach der Reihe!
Die Bogenlampe zischt zum Schluß nach Licht –
Wir schieben geil und gähnend uns ins Freie.

X
The End: Cinematograph

The hall goes dark. We see the rapids and falls
Of the Ganges, palms, temples raised to Brahma,
A silently raging family drama,
Men about town, and masquerade balls.

Revolvers are drawn in jealousy's wrath:
Mister Pipsqueak duels, and onlookers loiter.
An alpine peasant with pannier and goiter,
Bearing her load up the steepest path.

Through forests of larch lead her trails,
Then they twist below towering sheer
Rock cliffs. The view in the depths unveils
Piebald cattle, potato fields, and deer.

And in the darkened room – into my sight –
It flickers, horrific! This, that, and more!
The arc lamp fizzles *finis* in search of light –
We shuffle, lewd and yawning, out the door.

XI
Draußen

Die Sommernacht ist schwer nur zu ertragen!
Vier Herren gehn mit abgeknöpftem Kragen.
Ein Lackbeschuhter stellt der Schnepse nach …
Da polterts her – Ein langgedehnter Krach:
Der Donner!
Au!
Ist die Reklame plump,
Blitz!
Ein feiner Mensch liebt nicht den lauten Mum-
pitz!
Das klingt ja ganz, als ob der dicke nackte
Weltgeist
Ganz vertrackte Katarakte im Tackte knackte.

XI
Outside

This summer night is hard to take!
Four men (unbuttoned collars) are on the make.
A patent-leather shoed one stalks a floozy.
We hear a rumble – a long, drawn-out doozy
Of a crash: Thunder!
Ow!
If the ad's the crudest,
Add lightning bolts!
A cultivated man abhors the rudest
Foolish dolts!
It sounds as if the great world spirit – naked, fat –
Cracked and crapped compacted cataracts in tact.

Der Träumende

An Kay Heinrich Nebel

Blaugrüne Nacht, die stummen Farben glimmen.
Ist er bedroht vom roten Strahl der Speere
und rohen Panzern? Ziehn hier Satans Heere?
Die gelben Flecke, die im Schatten schwimmen,
sind Augen wesenloser großer Pferde.
Sein Leib ist nackt und bleich und ohne Wehre.
Ein fades Rosa eitert aus der Erde.

The Dreaming Man

to Kay Heinrich Nebel

Blue-green night, the silent colors gleam and glint.
Do crimson rays of spears cause panic?
Who marches here? Armored hosts satanic?
In shadow, yellow blotches squint
Like eyes of soulless horses of great girth.
His body's defenseless, naked, wan in tint.
A pale, pink pus oozes from the earth.

Der Tag der Stadt

Am Abend

Ach! die glitschig nasse Planke
War ihm mächtig unbequem.
Saß er doch auf einer Banke
Und bedachte ein Problem.

Dachte, dachte; er war wichtig
Denn er gab sich das Gebot:
»Löse jene Frage richtig
Oder mach dich, bitte, tot.«

In der Bülowstraße war es.
Ja, es war ein Abenteuer
Heldisch war und voll Gefahr es
Ward er dümmer? Ward er schläuer?

Ja! er saß auf einer Banke
Und er hatte ein Problem
Und die pitschenasse Planke
Ward ihm auch sehr unbequem.

The Day of the City

In the Evening

The board was dirty as a trench.
It tortured his behind.
He sat there on the bench
With a problem on his mind.

He thought and thought. A man to be heeded!
For he gave himself an order:
"Find the answer that's needed,
Or please, just kill yourself. No quarter!"

It was on Bülow Street:
An adventurous exploit,
A perilous, heroic feat.
Did he grow stupid? Or mentally adroit?

Yes, he sat there on a bench
With a problem on his mind
And the board as dirty as a trench
Tortured his behind.

Die Stadt

Ich sah den Mond und des ägäischen
Grausamen Meeres tausendfachen Pomp
All meine Pfade rangen mit der Nacht.

Doch sieben Fackeln waren mein Geleit
Durch Wolken glühend, jedem Sieg bereit.

»Darf ich dem Nichts erliegen, darf mich quälen
Der Städte weiten Städte böser Wind?
Da ich zerbrach den öden Tag des Lebens!«

Verschollene Fahrten! Eure Siege sind
Zu lange schon verflackt. Ah! helle Flöten
Und Geigen tönen meinen Gram vergebens.

The City

I saw the moon and the thousand-fold
Pomp of the gruesome Aegean Sea
All my paths grappled with the night

But seven torches escorted me
Through glowing clouds, prepared for every victory.

"May I succumb to nothingness, may I be racked
By the wicked wind of vastest cities?
Because I shattered life's joylessness!"

Lost, forgotten journeys! How time does tarnish
Your triumphs. Ah! A host of high-pitched flutes
And violins intone my grief, but all to no avail.

Der Traum

Jawohl! Wir träumen oft von großen Prünken
Und durch die goldene Stadt, als Triumphator
Kutschieren wir erhaben dem Senat vor
Und nackte Mädchen stehn auf Marmelstrünken.

Der Wagen fliegt den Vogelflug der Möwen
Trotzdem er köstlich teure Beute führt
Und diamantenes Geschirr umschnürt
Die Löwin und den Tibetaner-Löwen.

Da stürzt der Wagen. Plötzlich! Weh, verlieren
Die Löwen sich zu Wut der Wüstennächte
Weh! wer ist nahe der uns Hilfe brächte
Weh! in der Not! – Die Bestien coitieren.

The Dream

Oh yes! We dream the golden city's splendors grand,
We ride in triumph's chariot and raise our chalice.
On the street, crowds cheer us to the Senate's palace,
And naked girls are posed, each on a marble stand.

The wagon flies the way the seagulls soar,
Their precious booty weighs, but makes them glad.
Elaborate in diamond harnesses are clad
The lioness and lion from Tibet; they roar.

The wagon topples. Suddenly! Oh, woe! The lions lose
Themselves to all the wrath of desert night.
Woe! Who's near enough to help us in our plight?
Woe! The lions copulate and then they schmooze.

Am Morgen

Er spricht: »Nicht ängstlich an Gestaden
Auf offnem Meere will ich baden –
Ha! der Vergleich ist ein gewagter!
Ich werde frei vom Frohn der Zeiten
Zum kosmisch-schöpferischen schreiten.« –
(Kosmisch, sagt er.)
Er wandelt kühn um seinen Tisch, er wandelt
wohl die ganze Nacht
Beglückt in seiner Lampe Licht,
Das jetzt am Tag am Blau zerbricht.
Die ganze Nacht hat er umgebracht!
(So ein Kerl!)

In the Morning

He speaks: "Not meekly on the beaches
Will I bathe, but on the ocean's open reaches –
(Ha! The comparison's a stretch, but not absurd!)
Free from thrall to time and tide,
On to the cosmic-creative I shall stride!"
(Cosmic – his word.)
He circles boldly 'round his table, circles all the night,
Happy in his lamp's bright light
That now is broken by the blue of day.
(He's killed the night – it's done away!
What a guy!)

Der Oberlehrer

Gewaltig hockt er auf dem Tisch und spricht
Von Theben und Athen, heut nachmittag.
Ein grauer Schnurrbart starrt durch sein Gesicht
Er riecht nach saurem Brot und nach Tobak.

Sein kahles Haupt umwettert der Gedanke
Von Thebens heiliger Schaar, von Pindar spricht er
Der Primus reibt sich an der alten Banke
Die meisten machen willige Gesichter.

Er spricht von Theben heute nachmittag
Einige heben ihre kleinen Hände,
Einige kitzeln leise sich am Sack
Und gucken schläfrig auf die leeren Wände.

»Wer hat soeben auf den Tisch gehauen?«
Durch die betrübten Fenster schimmern Wolken.
Die Jungen sitzen staunend und verdauen. –
Der Lehrer wird jetzt in der Nase polken.

The Pedagogue

He's perched so mighty on the table, speaks today
Of Thebes and Athens. A stiff and perfect gent.
Through his face a moustache stares. It's gray.
Sour bread and pipe tobacco are his scent.

His balding pate is stormed by thought
Of Theban holy hosts and Pindar's lyric graces.
The teacher's pet? He rubs his favorite spot.
Most pupils put on willing faces.

He speaks of Thebes this afternoon,
And through the room raised hands are strewn,
While some are bored. They scratch their balls
And stare, lunch-sleepy, at the vacant walls.

"Who pounded on the table? Who's the pest?"
Clouds shimmer through the smudge-blurred windows.
The pupils sit, astonished, and digest.
The teacher's demonstration: how to pick your nose.

Italien

I

Laß ab mit Gesten trauriger Poeten
In Reim und Wohllaut sinnig zu verklingen,
Du brauchst auch nicht als schlauster der Asketen
Probleme lösend, nach Erlösung ringen.

Hier spreizen sich die keck zum Dom verpraßten
Rundbogen, Mosaiken, Marmorquasten.
Venedigs Lüfte kitzeln deine Haut.

Auf Säulchen tronen hier Geflügelgreife.
Steinerne Löwen heben ihre Schweife.
Ein Dampfer kommt und raucht und tutet laut.

Und leise staunend gondle durch die Buntheit,
Nur noch zu sanften Räuschen der Gesundheit
Sahst du am Lido tausend Weiber nackt?

O, lobe die Lagunen, die so stinken,
In süße Tage wirst du bald versinken
Vergnügt, Genießer, oft befrackt.

Italy

I

Leave off sounding out the gestures of pathetic
Poets in grand rhyme and melody profound;
You needn't seek, as cleverest ascetic,
To solve all problems or find salvation's ground.

Marble pom-poms and mosaics, pertly squandered
On the path to the cathedral where you've wandered,
The air of Venice tickling your skin;

Poultry griffins on a marble pillar throne;
Sculpted lions lift their tails of stone;
A steamer comes and smokes and toots: what din!

The gondola threads you through the colorful crowd.
You're astonished in the murmuring of health, not loud.
Did you see a thousand naked women on the Lido?

O praise the still lagoons and praise their stink!
So sweet the days in which you soon will sink
In delight, you connoisseur in your tuxedo.

II

So ward er klug und hat sich tief entzückt
An jedem Dinge, das ihn angeblickt.

An jedem Hauch, der ihn aus Gärten anweht,
An jedem Heldengauch, der ihn nichts angeht.

Am weißen Tag und purpurnen Geweben,
Und Bildern keusch und bunt, an Dunst und Tal,
An wilden Kirchen, wo die Engel schweben,
Am festgefügten schweigenden Portal!

Nun steht er da auf einem breiten Platze,
Und weiß nicht mehr: zu welchem Wunder wandern.
Die Häuser prunken eines wie die andern,
Die Sonne glüht als fette Feuerglatze.

Ja, hätt' ich Feinde zu endlosen Kämpfen,
Ließe mein Haß mich viele Straßen gehen.
Hat nicht den Teufel mit den Schwefeldämpfen
Sich Gott zum Zeitvertreib einst angestellt?

Er steht und grübelt, seine Sinne flehen:
Entdecke dir die Häßlichkeit der Welt.

II

He thus grew wise and found delights
In everything that had him in its sights:

In scents a-waft from leafy garden plots,
In each daft hero, though they concern him not,

In white of day and splendid crimson coats,
In haze and vale, in visions pied and chaste,
In feral churches where an angel floats,
In firmly-joined and silent gates, art-graced!

He stands on one of many spacious squares,
Not knowing to which wonder he should wander,
Or of which resplendent, rich palazzo to be fonder.
The sun, a fat, bald fiery pate, flares and glares.

If I had foes with whom an endless battle looms,
My hate would send me down not one, but every street.
Was not the Devil, with his evil sulfur fumes,
Employed by God as sport, a challenge we've been hurled?

He stands and broods and all his senses now entreat:
Discover for yourself how ugly is the world.

III

Doch ein Palast stand huldvoll in Florenz,
Er hob sich starr in steile Sonnengluten
Mit reichem runden, steinernen Gekränz,
Sein Tor verzierten wuchtige Voluten.

Er sprach: »O Mensch! du weißt doch, was wir lehren!
Gebildeter! schon Goethe hat erkannt es:
Wer wird das Leben unnütz sich erschweren!
Man stell sich auf und sei was Imposantes.

Du aber liebst dir das Geabenteure,
Du blickst bedenklich selbst zur schönsten Zinnung.
Lockt dich der Hohn der Zweifel und das Neure?
An meinen Quadern scheitre deine Sinnung.

Entschließe dich, auf Goethens Pfad zu schreiten
Mit Männertritt und würdig froh gelaunt!

Sein weißer Schlafrock glänzt durch die Gezeiten.«
Sprach der Palast. Ich war nicht schlecht erstaunt.

III

A palace stood in Florence with great dignity;
It rose up rigid in the sun, whose blaze was great,
With rich, round capitals in stony filigree,
And colossal volutes beautified its entry gate.

It spoke to me: "O Man! You know quite well our creed.
O highbrow! Even Goethe found it to his liking:
A life encumbered – who would seek it without need?
One rises up, becoming someone striking.

Of every bold adventure, you're a passionate pursuer;
On lovely crenellated battlements you cast a doubting eye.
Are you enticed by doubt's derision, by everything that's newer?
On my hewn stones, your vision fails; enduring, they defy.

Resolve yourself on Goethe's path to stride
With manly step and worthy cheer unfazed,

His dressing gown gleams white through time and tide,"
Thus spoke the palace. I was quite amazed.

IV

Der Mittag kam mit Staub und sehr viel Hitze,
Ich tat mich langsam auf das Kanapee.
Nun liegst du da, du stilisierter Fritze,
Das ist bequemer als am Gardasee
Landschaft zu schlürfen, oder zu Firenze
Die Hallen Michelozzos, Frühlingstänze
Des Sandro Botticelli oder sowas.
Ach bleib, ach bleib, Genießer, ohne Ende,
Zu schnarchen hier, im Lustrevier des Sofas!

Ich gähnte stolz. So stürze dich verwegen,
Toll, ja toll, mit jauchzendem Munde,
Den Kopf durch die Wände
Deinen gefährlichsten Wünschen entgegen.
So sprach zu mir die allerstillste Stunde.
Und kein Klavier, kein Baby hat
Geschrien im ganzen Haus.
Und die Sonne, die Sonne lag über der Stadt,
Und brütete Wanzen aus.

IV

Midday came with dust and temperatures high.
Slowly I settled on the restful settee.
Now you lie there, you stylized guy,
More comfortable than slurping sweaty
Landscapes at Lago de Garda, or in Florence the chance
To see the halls of Michelozzo or the vernal dance
Of Sandro Botticelli, or whatever painter pros.
Ah, epicure! Linger long in your trance
On your pleasure-garden sofa! Snore in repose!

I proudly yawned. So take a flier!
Mad, yes mad, with your exulting mouth,
Smash your head through walls, don't cower,
In quest of your most dangerous desire:
Thus spoke to me the silentest hour.
And no piano, no baby, no none,
Squalled in all the house.
Over the city lay the sun, the sun,
Hatching the eggs of the louse.

V

So waren wir auch in Italien Gäste,
Und haben dort so manchen Tag verschlafen.
Wir tranken Wein in Kinematographen,
Und krochen durch die Gärten und Paläste.

Und gaben manchmal uns den ungestümen
Fassaden hin, Gewölben und Kapellen,
Schlanken Pilastern und den ungetümen
Und dicken süßen Leibern in Bordellen.

V

Thus were we guests in Italy
And lazed away many a day in bed,
Drank wine in houses of cinematography,
Crept through gardens and palaces with throbbing head.

And at times, we opened ourselves to stormy
Facades, vaults, and chapels (we pious fellows),
Slender pilasters and, not to forget, those enormy,
Fat, sweet bodies cavorting in bordellos.

Legende

In Indien – sagt man – weint der Mond Kristalle,
Den schattenloser schwerer Traum umwand.
Und wer des Mondes Träne drunten fand,
Der geht gefeit vor Tod und jähem Falle.

Nun mag die Pest der Völker Leiber fretzen
Und Hunger sie auf Wegen müde hetzen.
Er aber quert die Nacht und die Gewimmer,
In Händen haltend nie versiegten Schimmer.

Legend

In India – they say – the moon weeps crystal,
Wrapped in shadowless and heavy dreams,
And he who finds these tears therein, it seems,
Will be immune to death and never wistful.

Now, the plague may gorge upon the bodies of the nations
And hunger hound the weary in their stations and migrations,
But that finder crosses night and all the whining
And holds in hands a never-ending shining.

Der Morgen des Philosophen

Er spricht: »Nicht ängstlich an Gestaden
Auf offnem Meere will ich baden
(Ha! der Vergleich ist ein gewagter!):
Ich werde frei vom Frohn der Zeiten
Zum kosmisch-schöpferischen schreiten.« –
(Kosmisch, sagt er.)
Er wandelt kühn um seinen Tisch, er wandelt schon
die ganze Nacht
Wohl in dem gelben Lampenlicht
Das jetzt am blauen Tag zerbricht
(Die ganze Nacht hat er umgebracht!
So ein Kerl!)

The Morning of the Philosopher

He speaks: “Not meekly on the beaches
Will I bathe, but on the ocean’s open reaches –
(Ha! The comparison’s a stretch, but not absurd!)
Free from thrall to time and tide,
On to the cosmic-creative I shall stride!”
(Cosmic – his word.)
He circles boldly ’round his table, circles all the night,
Happy in the yellow lamplight
That now is broken by the blue of day.
(He’s killed the night – it’s done away!
What a guy!)

Nacht

I

Und Schmock im Rock
Und Mann in Bart.
Jetzt in der Bar
Zu Paaren gepaart
Und bunter Plunder
Und Strümpfchen verflucht
Seid ihr das Wunder,
Das heut ich gesucht?

Wir suchten auf Straßen
Auf und ab. Auf und ab.
Wir standen und saßen
Und liefen im Trab.
Ganz über die Maßen
Erwartungsvoll
Jetzt ist das Lokal verjohlt und voll.

Night

I

And shmuck in a smock
And man in beard.
In the beer bar
Coupled to couples
And colorful baubles
And stockings be darned
Are you the wonder, now appeared,
That I sought from afar?

We searched every street
Up and down. All around.
We sat and we stood on our feet.
We moved at a trot.
Beyond every bound
Expecting a lot
Loud in the lounge: the crowd and its sound.

II

Es hebt sich ein rosa Gesicht
Von der Wand
Es strahlt ein verwegenes Licht
Von der Wand
Es kracht mir der Schädel
Beim Anblick der Wand
Es träumt mir ein Mädel
Beim Anblick der Wand.

O Wand, die in meine leblosen Stunden starrt
Wand, Wand, die meine Seele mit Wundern genarrt
Mit Langweile und grünlichem Kalk
Mein Freund. Meiner Wünsche Dreckkatafalk.

Soeben erscheint mir der Mond
An der Wand.
Es zeigt mir Herr Cohn seine Hand
An der Wand.
Es schnattert wie Schatten
Pretiös an der Wand.

Verflucht an der Wand!
Und heut an der Wand!
Was stehen denn so viel Leut
An der Wand?

II

A pink face comes into sight
From the wall
It beams a raffish light
From the wall
Sets my skull in a whirl
With the sight of the wall
I dream of a girl
Upon sight of the wall

O wall, staring into my lifeless hours
Wall, wall, that fools my soul with wondrous powers
With boredom and greenish whitewash chalk:
My friend. My wishes' dirt catafalque.

Just now, the sight of the moon's ball
On the wall
Shows me Herr Cohn's hand, fingers fanned
On the wall.
It prattles like shadows
Mannered on the wall.

Damned on the wall
Today against the wall!
Why are so many people, do say,
Standing against the wall?

III

Ja ich träume. Eine Tasse
Steht auf einem Tische rund,
Ach was ist denn diese crasse
Sache, die ich sehend hasse?
Tut sie nicht ein Wunder kund?!

Ja ich werde mich begnügen
Daß es solch ein Ding noch gibt
Das sich nicht mit Engelsflügen
Aufwärts hebt und fortbegibt.

Schließlich könnten Teller schweben
Stühle streckend alle vier
Beine aufwärts wie Epheben
Gott, mein Gott, ich danke Dir.

III

Yes, I'm dreaming. A glass
Stands on a table, round.
Oh, what then is this crass
Thing my gaze hates when it's found?
Doesn't its annunciation astound?

Yes, I'll be quite content
If there still are such things
That didn't spread angel wings
And rise up and that nowhere went.

After all, plates could float, suspended
Chairs extend all four
Legs like recruits, upended
God, my God, I thank you evermore.

IV

Man fühlt sich dreckig und verlaust
Und träumt verwegen in den Morgenradau
Ein altes Weib hat auch gesungen
Wiegend die Brust. Ein Lockruf der Liebe.

Was war er früher so wohlvertraut
Der kranke Schimmel – vom Fenster aus
Heut trübt er mir die Abgedanken.
Ein grauer Wirbel. Man gähnt und träumt.

Vom gestrigen Abend, dem Tatenheld
Der Auto tückisch ins Zimmer schrie
Sterne wie Frauen und lumpige Stunden
Hat mir der schlampige Herr versprochen.

Nun bin ich dreckig und fast verlaust
und steige betrübt in den Morgenzug.
Ein Philosoph hat auch geredet
Wiegend die Brust. Ein liebreicher Herr.

IV

One feels dirty and lice-infested
And dreams raffishly in the morning racket.
An old woman sang, too,
Rocking her breast. Mating call of love.

Oh, how familiar it once was
The sick mildew – from out the window
Today it clouds my resigned thoughts.
A gray eddy. One yawns and dreams.

Of yesterday evening, the action hero
Who, shrewd, shouted into the room. "Car!"
Stars like women and a few tattered hours
The grubby gentleman promised me.

Now I am dirty and near lice-infested
And climb, gloomy, onto the morning train.
A philosopher, too, spoke
Rocking his breast. An affectionate gentleman.

Der Freund

Ich stieß den Dolch ihm in die Eingeweide –
Am Boden standen blanke Pfützen Blut.
Eh war noch Lärm, jetzt hüllt uns Schweigen beide.
Ich staunte wie ein Kind. Denn von der Wut
Des Suchens nach verlornen Paradiesen
War jede Kunde tot. Der Mittag dehnte
Sich selig auf der Höfe kahlen Fliesen.
Gewaltig war der Tag, wie ihn sein toter Freund ersehnte.

The Friend

Deep into his guts I rammed the blade.
Bare pools of blood made the ground a stage.
Clamor fades; around us, a swath of silence now is laid.
I stood in awe like a child. From the rage
Of searching long for paradises lost,
Each message died. Midday stretched and burned
The naked courtyard tiles, blithe, light-embossed.
O! Mighty was the day – for which his dead friend yearned.

Klage

Wird denn die Sonne alle Träume morden,
Die blassen Kinder meiner Lustreviere?
Die Tage sind so still und grell geworden
Erfüllung lockt mit wolkigen Gesichten.
Mich packt die Angst, daß ich mein Heil verliere.

Wie wenn ich ginge, meinen Gott zu richten.

Lament

Will the sun, then, murder every dream,
Each pale child of my pleasure precinct?
The days have grown so still in garish gleam,
Fulfillment beckons with faces indistinct.
I'm filled with fear I'll lose salvation.

As if I went to sentence God to His damnation.

Die Himmelsschlange

Sonne glüht und Nächte schweigen,
Aus den hellen Fenstern steigen
Die Gespenster,
Unzucht treibend
In der Luft.
Und die Stadt
Verhüllt der Duft
Ihrer Schnapsgesichter.

»Laßt uns durch die großen Hallen
Der betörten Himmel wallen;
Denn der Mond ist doch schon fern.
Es verglomm der Grimm der Sterne.
Ist es Funkel, ist es dunkel,
Ist es Sang, Gebet, Gemunkel,
Sind's Paläste oder Plunder?
Schweigt, wir sind im Reich der Wunder.«

Hunderttausend Heere ziehen
Durch die Wolkenplane.
Hunderttausend Freunde fliehen
Vor der Wolken Karawane.
Ach, dem Denker wird es übel,
Der das Heut' bedenken soll.
Steckt ihn in den Wasserkübel.
Er ist toll.

Die Wolken winden sich wie Leinentuch,
Im Himmel spür' ich gräßliche Exzesse.

The Heavenly Serpent

Sun glows tempestuously
And nights go hush,
From radiant windows ghosts rise
Coupling incestuously
In the breeze.
And the city
Veils the fragrance
Of their whiskey faces.

"Let us flutter through the great halls
Of the befuddled heavens;
For the moon is already distant.
It quelled the wrath of stars.
Does it sparkle, is it dark and dingy,
Is it song, prayer, stingy
Innuendo? Are those palaces or plunder?
Be still, we're in the realm of wonder."

A hundred thousand hosts are sweeping
Through the billowing cloud cavalcade.
A hundred thousand friends are fleeing
The cumulo-nimbus cascade.
Alas, the wise man who ponders deep enough
This day and age will get queasy.
Dunk him in the water trough.
He's crazy.

Clouds wriggle and writhe like sheets in the breezes,
I sense ghastly excesses in heaven – no joke.

Die Engel fürchten sich vor Gottes Fluch
Und haben Zigaretten in der Fresse.

Denn Luzifer ist heute eingeladen
Und geht mit einem sicherlich zu Bett.
Durch sieben Himmel zieht in dicken Schwaden
Dampf von Tabak und Armesünder-Fett.

The curse of God has scared the living bejesus
Out of the angels, who toke a holy smoke.

Lucifer got an invite and it caused quite a hubbub
For he's off to bed with a puffy-cheeked cherub.
Tobacco fumes and the fat of death-row felons
Waft in thick swaths all through the seven heavens.

Der Teufel spricht:

»Ein alter Leichnam kriecht aus seinem Loche
Im Eisenkleid nach alter Krieger Art.
Er tut es jeden Sonntag in der Woche.
Die Glocke dröhnt. Im Winde weht sein Bart.
Zum Morde hebt er die verfallne Linke,
Ihr wißt ja nicht, wie wohl das Geistern tut.
Mit seiner Rechten macht er Winke-Winke.
Aus sieben Wunden strömt er Rauch und Glut.«

Ein kleiner Engel knaut und will nicht essen.
Fürwahr! Er hat den Teufel so geliebt.
Doch jetzt beschließt er, seiner zu vergessen.
Da er ihm nicht mal 'ne Zigarre gibt.
Doch jener sieht ihn an mit blassen Blicken.
Und freut sich sehr, daß sich der Kleine kränkt.
»Wie werden wir uns heute Nacht erquicken,
Doch die Zigarre kriegst'te nicht geschenkt.«

Im Saale weiße Fliegenschwärme.
Der Dunst von Wein schlägt aus dem Mund der Zecher.
Im Saale taumeln weiße Fliegenschwärme,
Berauscht vom Zorn und vom Atem der Zecher.
Berauscht vom Atem der Zecher Scharen weißer Fliegen.

Schwirren wie verrückte Tanten
Zu Bekannten
Und Folianten
Und zu unbekannten Kanten,
Schnatternd auf der Eisenbahn.

The Devil Speaks:

"An ancient corpse crawls from its crypt
Garbed like some aged warrior in chain mail.
He does this every Sunday, according to script:
The bell bongs. He rises up, beard blowing in the gale,
A decayed left hand raised, ready to smite,
(No one knows the joy of a ghost making rounds)
While his right waves bye-bye, ta-ta, nighty-night.
Smoke and glowing embers stream from seven wounds."

A tiny angel whinges, doesn't want to eat. Verily,
Verily, I say unto you, he doted on the devil,
But now decides to forget him momentarily
For begrudging him a cigar with which to revel.
But the devil looks at him with blank stares
And is happy that the little one is miffed.
"We'll revive ourselves tonight and put on airs,
But still it's no cigar: you get no gift."

White swarms of flies in the saloon.
Vapor of the grape wafts from the mouths of winos.
White swarms of flies stagger through the saloon,
Drunk with anger and the breath of lushes.
Drunk from the breath of the drinkards' posse of white flies.

Buzzing about like crazy aunties
In their panties
Waving hankies
While dandies
Are cackling in the shanties by the railroad.

Siehste woll!
Der Mann ist toll.
Seine Nase glüht und thront
Durch die Dünste wie der Mond,
Wenn er aufgeht.
Ob er, schrecklich zugerichtet,
Immer unerhörter dichtet,
Bis er draufgeht?

Ich rauch die Zigarette
Und geh im Zimmer rum.
Der Teppich ist so kokette,
Ihn ziert gar manche Blum.

Der Mond ist meine Tante,
Er schmoddert durch die Nacht.
Die Sonne, meine Großmama,
Hat nie an mich gedacht.

Don't you see?! The man has loaned
Out his sanity.
His nose glows and sits enthroned
In the haze beneath his eyes
Like a bloodshot moon on the rise.
After taking such a flogging,
Will he continue with his mind-boggling
Versifying until he dies?

I smoke a cigarette
And walk around the room.
The carpet's such a cute coquette,
Adorned with many a bloom.

The moon is my aunt,
It sludges through the night.
The sun, my grandmama,
Never gave me a thought.

Der Todesengel

I

Mit Trommelwirbeln geht der Hochzeitszug,
In seid'ner Sänfte wird die Braut getragen,
Durch rote Wolken weißer Rosse Flug,
Die ungeduldig gold'ne Zäume nagen.

Der Todesengel harrt in Himmelshallen
Als wüster Freier dieser zarten Braut.
Und seine wilden, dunklen Haare fallen
Die Stirn hinab, auf der der Morgen graut.

Die Augen weit, vor Mitleid glühend offen
Wie trostlos starrend hin zu neuer Lust,
Ein grauenvolles, nie versiegtes Hoffen,
Ein Traum von Tagen, die er nie gewußt.

The Angel of Death

I

Drum roll. The wedding procession begins.
Resplendent in a silk sedan, the bride now sits,
Carried through red clouds of ivory stallions
Chomping at their glittering, gold-plated bits.

The angel of death waits in heaven's halls.
A savage suitor of this tender bride, he shakes
His head and wild, dark, unbridled hair falls
Down his furrowed brow, on which a new day breaks.

His piercing gaze transfixed, wide eyes afire,
His grief-stricken pity full blown:
A gruesome, never quenched desire,
A dream of days he's never known.

II

Er kommt aus einer Höhle, wo ein Knabe
Ihn als Geliebte wunderzart umfing.
Er flog durch seinen Traum als Schmetterling
Und ließ ihn Meere sehn als Morgengabe.

Und Lüfte Indiens, wo an Fiebertagen
Das greise Meer in gelbe Buchten rennt.
Die Tempel, wo die Priester Cymbeln schlagen,
Um Öfen tanzend, wo ein Mädchen brennt.

Sie schluchzt nur leise, denn der Schar Gesinge
Zeigt ihr den Götzen, der auf Wolken thront
Und Totenschädel trägt als Schenkelringe,
Der Flammenqual mit schwarzen Küssen lohnt.

Betrunkne tanzen nackend zwischen Degen,
Und einer stößt sich in die Brust und fällt.
Und während blutig sich die Schenkel regen,
Versinkt dem Knaben Tempel, Traum und Welt.

II

He leaves a cave where a young boy, not shy,
Sent tender embraces to him in a shower.
This lad then flew through his dream, a butterfly,
With visions of the sparkling seas his morning dower.

And the balmy breezes of India where, on days of chills
And fever, the senile sea flows into yellow bays.
And in the sacred temple, priests strike cymbals,
Dancing 'round an oven where a maid is set ablaze.

She sobs but softly, for the rabble sings
To point her to the idol on its cloudy throne;
It wears bare skulls as ankle rings:
Rewarding flaming agony with black kisses sown.

Bare-assed drunkards dance betwixt swords. What noise
As one stabs himself in the chest and falls. While blood-
Stained shanks thrash violently about, the young boy's
Temple, dream, and world sink, silent, into mud.

III

Dann flog er hin zu einem alten Manne
Und kam ans Bett als grüner Papagei.
Und krächzt das Lied: »O schmähliche Susanne!«
Die längst vergeßne Jugendlitanei.

Der stiert ihn an. Aus Augen glasig blöde
Blitzt noch ein Strahl. Ein letztes böses Lächeln
Zuckt um das zahnlose Maul. Des Zimmers Öde
Erschüttert jäh ein lautes Todesröcheln.

III

Then off he flew as an emerald-green parrot
To an old man's sleeping booth.
And squawked "A Tale of Knights-Errant",
The long-forgotten litany of youth.

The gnarled old man stares at him. Glassy, weary
Eyes flash a malicious twinkle, as senseless brabble
Twitches from his toothless grin until the dreary
Room is rocked by a deafening death rattle.

IV

Die Braut friert leise unterm leichten Kleide.
Der Engel schweigt. Die Lüfte ziehn wie krank.
Er stürzt auf seine Knie. Nun zittern beide.
Vom Strahl der Liebe, der aus Himmeln drang.

Posaunenschall und dunkler Donner lachen.
Ein Schleier überflog das Morgenrot.
Als sie mit ihrer zärtlichen und schwachen
Bewegung ihm den Mund zum Küssen bot.

IV

Under her light gown, the bride feels a chill; she's quivering.
The angel is silent. Balmy breezes turn to a sickly draft, the sky
Darkens as he falls to his knees. Now both are shivering
From the ray of love piercing down from on high.

Trumpet flourish. Dark thunder laughs bleakly.
The blood-red sky is veiled at sunrise
As she gingerly moves so tender, yet weakly,
Offering him her lips full on as his prize.

Andante

Auf blühen Papierwiesen
Leuchtend und grün
Da stehen drei Kühe
Und singen kühn:

»O Wälder, o Wolken
»O farbige Winde
»Wir werden gemolken
»Geschwinde, geschwinde …

»In goldene Eimer
»Fließt unser Saft
»In farbige Reimer
»Ergießt unsere Kraft

»Wir stehen hier, im Chor beisammen,
»Auf knotigem Beine
»Und die Kräfte der Erde sind
»Angesammelt zu frohem Vereine.«

Sie bocken bei Tag und sie trillern bei Nacht.

Andante

Paper meadows unfold in bloom
Glowing and green,
Three cows are standing there
They sing, they keen:

"O forests, o cloudy mists!
"O colorful zephyrs!
"We're milked by skilled fists,
"Quick, be quick," call the heifers...

"Into buckets of gold
"We pour out our juice,
"Rhymers catch and hold
"The force we let loose.

"We stand together, a choir
"On bony legs at the hub
"Of the world's powers entire,
"Convened as a celebrant club."

They rut by day and warble by night.

Zweifel

Da diese Nächte uns nur Morgen sind
Für Feuertage, die wir nicht erkennen,
Darf ich in trüber Luft, als blödes Kind,
Verängstigt noch um Liebesstunden flennen.

Schon zucken Stadt und Meer vor Himmelssöhnen,
Die ihre ersten Zornespfeile senden,
Im Lampenlicht schon Helle; dieses Dröhnen
Verlorner Nächte spricht von Mittagsbränden.

Despair

For us, these nights are mornings that prepare
For fiery days beyond our vision's powers.
So I, a silly child in gloomy air,
May, anxious, whine for happy trysting hours.

Already sea and city flinch before
The sons of heaven's arrows, tipped with ire
Beneath the lamplight, glare; this booming roar
Of long-lost nights that speak of noontime fire.

Hymne

O Traum, Verdauung meiner Seele!
Elendes combination womit ich vor Frost mich schütze!
Zerstörer aller Dinge die mir feind sind;
Aller Nachttöpfe,
Kochlöffel und Litfaßsäulen …
O du mein Schießgewehr.

In purpurne Finsternis tauchst du die Tage
Alle Nächte bekommen violette Horizonte
Meine Großmama Pauline erscheint als Astralleib
Und sogar ein Herr Satanitätsrat
Ein braver aber etwas zu gebildeter
Sanitätsrat
Wird mir wieder amüsant
Er taucht auf aus seiner epheuumwobenen Ruhestätte
– War es nicht soeben ein himmelblauer Ofenschirm

(He Sie da!)
Und gackt: »Sogar …
(Frei nach Friedrich von Schiller)

O Traum, Verdauung meiner Seele
O du mein Schießgewehr.
Gick! Gack.

Hymn

O dream, digestion of my soul!
Miserable combination to protect myself from frost!
Destroyer of all things inimicable to me.
All chamberpots,
Cooking spoons, and billboard pillars…
Oh, you my gunnery.

You dip the days in purple shadows.
All nights receive violet horizons.
My grandmama Pauline appears as an astral body,
And even Mr. Member of the Board of Health,
A decent but somewhat too well educated
Member of the Board of Health,
I once more find amusing,
Arising from his ivy-covered resting place
– Wasn't that just a sky-blue fire-screen

(Hey you there!)
And cackles: "Even…
(Adapted from Friedrich von Schiller)

Oh dream, digestion of my soul!
Oh you my gunnery.
Look! Cackle.

Couplet

Bladdy Groth
War ein Mädchen von zartem Geblüt,
Bladdy Groth, Bladdy Groth ist tot.
Bladdy Groth war ein Mädchen von keuschem Geblüt
Und sie hat doch für viele Männer geglüht
Und keiner hat sich umsonst gemüht
Bladdy Groth, Bladdy Groth, Bladdy Groth.

Und sie sang, und sie spielte und tanzte zur Nacht
Und sie hat mich dort öfters ausgelacht
Bladdy Groth, Bladdy Groth ist tot.

Und was haben wir alles mit ihr nicht gemacht
Und sie hat sich doch gar nichts dabei gedacht
Bladdy Groth, Bladdy Groth, Bladdy Groth.

Und ihr Nacken, er war wie von Küssen verzehrt
Und sie hat sich doch vor niemand gewehrt
Bladdy Groth, Bladdy Groth, Bladdy Groth.
Und die Augen, die schossen Blitze blau
Und ihr Kleid war meistens auch himmelblau
Und heut ist zu der Engel Frau
Bladdy Groth, Bladdy Groth, Bladdy Groth.
Ah, wie werden die geflügelten Lucifere ihr zusehn,
Wenn sie mit den Engeln tengelntateratata.
Ob es im Himmel, Bladdy Groth! Bladdy Groth!
Wohl Sekt gibt?

Couplet

Bladdy Groth
Was a maid of gentle blood,
Bladdy Groth, Bladdy Groth is dead.
Bladdy Groth was a maid of virtuous blood.
And for many men, oh how she glowed.
And no man's effort was a dud.
Bladdy Groth, Bladdy Groth, Bladdy Groth.

And she sang, and she played and danced all night,
And often she would jeer at my plight.
Bladdy Groth, Bladdy Groth is dead.

And didn't we all do with her as we might?
Whatever second thoughts she had were slight.
Bladdy Groth, Bladdy Groth, Bladdy Groth.

Her neck was devoured by kisses
Everyone aims for her; nobody misses
Bladdy Groth, Bladdy Groth, Bladdy Groth.
And her eyes, they shot lightning bolts blue,
And her dress was most often sky-blue, too.
And today, she to the angels flew.
Bladdy Groth, Bladdy Groth, Bladdy Groth.
Ah, how the winged Lucifers will look at her
When she ting-a-lingle-lings with the angels.
Bladdy Groth! Bladdy Groth! Does heaven
Serve champagne?

Morgens

Ein starker Wind sprang empor.
Öffnet des eisernen Himmels blutende Tore.
Schlägt an die Türme.
Hellklingend laut geschmeidig über die eherne Ebene der Stadt.
Die Morgensonne rußig. Auf Dämmen donnern Züge.
Durch Wolken pflügen goldne Engelpflüge.
Starker Wind über der bleichen Stadt.
Dampfer und Krähne erwachen am schmutzig fließenden Strom.
Verdrossen klopfen die Glocken am verwitterten Dom.
Viele Weiber siehst du und Mädchen zur Arbeit gehn.
Im bleichen Licht. Wild von der Nacht. Ihre Röcke wehn.
Glieder zur Liebe geschaffen.
Hin zur Maschine und mürrischem Mühn.
Sieh in das zärtliche Licht.
In der Bäume zärtliches Grün.
Horch! Die Spatzen schrein.
Und draußen auf wilderen Feldern
singen Lerchen.

Mornings

A strong wind sprang high.
Opens the blood-letting gates of the iron sky.
Strikes against the towers.
Loudly ringing, supple, high-pitched, over the brazen
plain of the city.
The morning sun sooty. On the causeway, trains thunder.
Golden angel plowshares plowing clouds asunder.
Strong wind over the pale city.
Steamboats and cranes awake when the turbid stream rolls.
In the weather-worn cathedral, a bell sullenly tolls.
Women and girls on the way to earn their bread and butter.
In the pale light. Wild from the night. Their skirts aflutter.
Limbs destined for love.
Off to the machine and tedious routine.
Gaze into the tender light.
Into the trees' tender green.
Hark! The sparrows shriek.
And off in the distant virgin fields,
Larks are singing.

Karthago

Der eherne Stier speit Flammen. Durchs offene Tempeldach
Blitzern die Strahlen der Sonne.
Männer mit offenen Armen beten.
Einer verschwand in dem krachenden dampfenden ehernen Maul –
Knabenmänner, die zum Tanz sich drehten.

O blaue Tage, Tage der blutigen Rosen,
Wo die bewaffneten Kähne die ewig bewegliche See durchschnitten.
Tage des Opfers und menschenmordender Bitten.
Wo die beschnittenen Priester mit sanft gleitenden Schritten
In den Winkeln der Gärten mit Frauen kosen.
Als Weib mit dem Weibe.
Und es zittern und klirren die Goldgeschmeide
Am heiligen Leibe.

Tage der purpurnen Sonnenstrahlen.
Tage der Glut in der steinernen Stadt.
Tage der Liebe und Tage der Qualen.
Tage des Zorns in der totwunden Stadt.

Über der blau donnernden Flut unermüdlicher Meere
Droht dir der Tod.
Hoch am Himmel steht der Komet bluteiternd und rot,
Ein Schwert, das die Leiber verzehrt,
Ein Drache der Wut.
Blut bedeutet das träumende Licht in den Straßen,
Vernichtung und Blut.
Umsonst heult der eherne Stier mit feurigem Schlunde,
Eure Töchter und Söhne verbrennt ihr im gräßlichen
Feuer vergebens.
Horch, es klingt der gläserne Tod durch die wüste Stunde.
Und es erstarrt im Mittagswunder der Traum und die Kraft
eures Lebens.

CARTHAGE

The bronze bull spews flames. Sunbeams flash
Through the temple's open roof.
Men pray with arms spread wide.
One vanished in the banging, steaming, brazen maw –
In dance, young men gyrate and glide.

O blue days, days of bloodshot roses,
Where battle-ready boats cut through the ever-churning seas.
Days of victims and homicidal pleas.
Where circumcised priests do a soft shoe, strike poses
In the corners of the garden, and cuddle with damsels,
As woman to woman.
All aquiver, the gold jewelry jingle-jangles
On the beatific body.

Days of crimson sunbeams.
Days of fervor in the lithic city.
Days of love and excruciating screams.
Days of anger in the death-doomed city.

Over the thundering blue flood of relentless seas,
Fate threatens to strike you dead.
High in the sky, the comet appears, blood-festering and red,
A sword that devours all flesh,
A raging dragon of ire.
Blood means light lost in a trance,
Carnage in the streets and more blood.
The bronze bull howls in vain with gaping maw ablaze,
You burn your sons and daughters on the funeral pyre, to no avail.
Hark, vitreous death rings through the desolate hour;
lives are torn asunder
And their dream and power congeal in the noontime wonder.

Tohub

Drei Männlein singen in der Höhe
Den gräßlichen Gesang:
Hast de Wanzen, Läuse, Flöhe,
Wird die Zeit dir gar nicht lang.

Immer hast de was zu knacken,
Es krabbelt hier und da.
Darfst packen und darfst zwacken –
O je! Halleluja!

Was soll die Langeweile,
Wo edel du verkommst.
Minute wird zur Meile,
Du siehst nur Zeit und brommst.

Auf dem Schädel hörst du die Haare,
Hinter den Ohren wächst dir Gras,
Dein Kiefer wird zur Knarre,
Schwer ächzend durch die Jahre
Auf und ab ohn' Unterlaß.

Drei Männlein singen in der Höhe
Den gräßlichen Gesang:
Hast du Wanzen, Läuse, Flöhe,
Wird dir die Zeit nicht lang.

Sie stiegen auf im Morgenrot
Und sangen Tag und Nacht,
Und störten Mittag- und Abendbrot
Und Luft und Erde kracht.

Tohub

Three little men are singing in the heights
They sing a gruesome song:
If you've got bedbugs, fleas, and lice,
Then you ain't got long.

Scrambling here and there, you say
There'll always be bugs to crack. How peculiar.
Pinching and grabbing what you may –
Oops! Oh dear! Hallelujah!

What's the point of being bored
When you go to ruin so nobly and divine.
Minute turns to mile, strikes a familiar chord.
You see nothing but time 'cause you're doin' time.

You hear hair sprouting on your skull,
Grass grows behind your ears,
Your jaw becomes your pistol,
Moaning heavily through the years
Utterly interminable.

Three little men are singing in the heights
They sing a gruesome song:
If you've got bedbugs, fleas, and lice,
Then you've not got long.

They rose up in the red of dawn
And sung through day and night,
Delaying lunch and supper too, whereupon
Earth and air crack with fright.

Der Visionarr

Lampe blöck nicht.
Aus der Wand fuhr ein dünner Frauenarm.
Er war bleich und blau geädert.
Die Finger waren mit kostbaren Ringen bepatzt.
Als ich die Hand küßte, erschrak ich:
Sie war lebendig und warm.
Das Gesicht wurde mir zerkratzt.
Ich nahm ein Küchenmesser und zerschnitt ein paar Adern.
Eine große Katze leckte zierlich das Blut vom Boden auf.
Ein Mann indes kroch mit gesträubten Haaren
Einen schräg an die Wand gelegten Besenstiel hinauf.

The Fool's Vision

Lamp don't bleat.
A woman's thin arm drove out of the wall.
It was pale and blue-veined.
The fingers splotched with precious rings.
As I kissed the hand, I shuddered:
It was alive and warm.
It scratched at my face. That stings.
I took a kitchen knife and sliced a couple of veins.
A huge cat daintily licked the blood from the floor.
While a man with spiked hair crawled up a broom
Handle obliquely propped against the wall.

Indianisch Lied

Lotte Pritzel gewidmet

Jetzt, Mädchen, sattle mein weißes Pferd,
Ein Ritt, da der Nachtmahr den Mond bedrängt,
Durch das dampfende Tal, da am Hexenherd
Der Freund der Indianer am Galgen hängt.

Zwölf Rosse brachen unter mir zusammen.
Zwölf Sonnen stürzten in den reißenden Strom ihre Flammen.
Doch am dreizehnten Tag um Mitternacht
Stand ich vor dem Toten und habe gelacht.

Ich blase die wütenden Totenfanfaren.
Armer versoffener Freund, nun bist du gestorben!
Ich bin der Indianer, der einst mit dir ritt,
Auf manchem Kriegspfad nahmst du mich mit
und wir haben die Länder und Leute verdorben,
und ich halt die Trompet und blas,
Faule Leiche, was grinst du so »monoise«,
Wo ich siebzehn mal vom Galgen dich schnitt?
Ist meine Lust am Leben dir immer noch leid?

Doch der trampt auf im Galgentritt:
Nu, warum blust de die Trompeit?

Jetzt baut man Ton des Weltgerichts,
Und der Geist in den Lüften schreit.
Doch du wohnst, wohin du dich sehntest, im Nichts,
Und es tönt in den Höhen der Satansritt.

Indian Song
dedicated to Lotte Pritzel

Saddle up my white horse, girl! Now! Let's go
For a ride! A nightmare haunts the moon, that's why!
Through the steaming valley, because at the witch's cauldron –
O Look! The Indians' friend swings from the gallows, high.

Twelve stallions collapsed under me. Their flames agleam,
Twelve suns nosedived into the rip-roaring stream.
Yet on the thirteenth day at the stroke of midnight
I stood before the dead man and laughed with delight.

I blow the raging fanfares of the dead.
Poor drunken friend, now you have died!
I am the Indian who once with you did ride;
On many a warpath you took me along,
And we ravaged countries and did people wrong,
And I hold the trumpet to blow like thunder –
Rotting corpse, why do you grin in wonder,
Where seventeen times on the gallows I cut you loose?
Does my lust for life still leave you forlorn?

But up he tromps to the gallows noose:
Well, why were you blowin' yer horn?

Now they're building the sound of Judgment Day,
And the spirit strides across the sky.
Yet you live in the void where you longed to stay,
And Satan's ride echoes on high.

Doch der trampt auf im Galgentritt:
Nu, warum blust de die Trompeit?

Du nanntest dich Pumperpuckel auf Erden,
»Denn man muß als häßlicher Satan erscheinen«.
Schüsse in Kneipen und Diebstahl von Pferden,
Schmutziges Stöhnen in Häusern aus Steinen,
Lächelnde Tage und ruchloses Weinen,
Armselige Täuschung, die ich erlitt.
Pumperpuckel, du hattest Einen.
Hinter den Wolken das Mondlicht schreit.

Doch der trampt auf im Galgentritt:
Nu, warum blust de die Trompeit?

Du, Schulmeister, sagtest: »Du denkst nur in Worten,
Doch alle Worte sind Trug nur und Leid.
Du, du denkst nur in Worten, in Taten und Orten,
Da der Gott aller Wahrheit dein Reden bestritt,
Und der Unsinn den Weg alles Sinnens verschneit.«
Ich denke nicht Worte und rede doch mit,
Und der Traum meines Daseins träumt Wahrheit und Traum.
Das bleibt doch ein prächtiger Galgenschnitt,
Was bleibst du nur hängen am hölzernen Baum,
Wie sehr ich dich bitte: komm mit, komm mit?
Heil! der geflügelte Morgenwind öffnete die
Himmelspforten des Lebens weit!

Doch der trampt auf im Galgentritt:
Nu, warum blust de die Trompeit?

But up he tromps to the gallows noose:
Well, why were you blowin' yer horn?

You named yourself Pumperpuckel under the sun,
"For one must appear as ugly as Satan, full blown."
Shoot up saloons, steal horses, then run.
Grimy groaning in houses of stone,
Smiling days and heinous weeping profuse,
Pathetic deceit I suffered it seems.
Pumperpuckel, you had a special papoose.
Behind the clouds the moonlight screams.

But up he tromps to the gallows noose:
Well, why were you blowin' yer horn?

You, pedant, once said: "You only think in words and phrases,
Yet, all words are nothing but lies, fraud, and woe.
You, you think only in words, in deeds and places,
Since the God of all truth says your speech is deluded,
Utter nonsense blankets all senses with snow."
I do not think words, but in pow-wows I'm included,
And the dream of my being dreams dream and veracity.
But wasn't it grand, how I cut you free?
So why are you still hanging on the wooden tree,
Oh, how I bid you: come along. Let's vamoose
Hail! the wingéd wind opens wide life's pearly gates:
a new morn!

But up he tromps to the gallows noose:
Well, why were you blowin' yer horn?

Einen schallenden Gruß meinem alten Freund!
Ein fester Galgen hält gut.
Und wenn herbstlicher Strahl unsere Ebenen träumt
Und den Vortraum des Winters in Zelten räumt,
Viel Feuer, Wasser und Mut.
Doch der weißen Rose vergesse ich nie,
Die auf schwarzen Rossen einst kam.
Denn sie zwang ihren Krieger aufs zitternde Knie
Und der Pfeil am Bogen ward lahm,
Welt vergessen und Träume verhöhnen,
Tode verachten im Walde der Tiere.
Doch wie kann ich vergessen ein Lächeln der Schönen,
Ihrer Augen nackte Wildheit und ihre
Unberührte Brust!
Jener Brand von Schönheit, der täglich die Welt verwirrt,
Jene schattenhafte Trauer, die um meinen Wigwam abenteuert.
Giftige Pfeile von der Rose der Brenta entsandt.
Warum kennt mich der Tod und lockt mich vergebens?
Warum bin ich heiter, wenn über endlosem Land
Die dröhnende Sonne verbrennt wie am sagenhaften
Abend des verendenden Lebens?

O Nacht zärtlicher Sterne Gefunkel
In liebesklarer Luft
Lebendigen Traumes Flammendunkel.
Über schmalen Wegen der Bergeskluft,
Hoch im Gebirg' in den eisigen Gipfeln ein Raunen.
Musik der Seele. Tanz und Märchen erstaunen.

A resounding greeting to my old friend!
A firm gallows holds fast.
When autumn's beam dreams our plains, and at last
Drives winter's premonition into the teepee,
So much fire, water, and audacity.
Forever in memory I'll see
The white rose: on black steeds it came.
For it forced the warrior to a trembling knee
And the arrow on his bow went limp and lame,
Forgetting the world and mocking fantasy,
Despising deaths in the forest of beasts.
Yet I cannot forget the beauty who smiled,
The naked fury of her wild eyes and, not least,
Untouched breast!
Yonder blaze of beauty leaves the world beguiled.
Yonder shadowy sadness circles my wigwam,
seeks adventure that's wild.
Poisoned arrows dispatched from the rose of Brenta fall like rain.
Why does death recognize and entice me in vain?
Why am I cheerful, when over endless prairie, round the bend,
The droning sun burns on that fabled evening
when life comes to an end?

O night of delicate stars, sparkling
In air as clear as love's kiss,
A living dream's flaming darkness.
Over narrow paths in the mountain's abyss,
High among stark, icy peaks, murmured in trance,
Hark! Music of the soul! Wondrous fable and dance!

Mehr als zu sein und mehr als nicht zu sein!
Wer darf den Leib denn denken, den er liebt!
Wer darf vermessen durch die Wälder schrein,
Daß Gott ihm nie den Tag der Schönheit gibt?
Farbiger Rauch steigt auf aus den Städten der Qual,
Wo der weiße Bruder bedächtig die Tonpfeife raucht,
Wie ein Feuer von Fieberträumen hingehaucht,
Fern am lauernden Horizont.

More than to be and more than not to be!
Who may ponder the body that sets eyes a-beaming?
Who may run through the forests, brashly screaming
That God never gives him his day of beauty to see?
Colorful smoke spirals up from cities teeming
With agony, where the white brother calmly sighs and
Puffs the peace pipe, like a fire feverishly dreaming,
Far off on the lurking horizon.

Gedichte aus dem Nachlass
Poems from the Literary Estate

Aus blauen Wunden glomm die müde Nacht
Und alle Straßen lagen ohne Scham
Und alle Fahnen schrieen in den Wind:
So geht ein Tag zur Neige.

Der glühte so, daß ich die Büßereide
Verschmähte und der Engel starre Glut.
Zu süß war diese Qual. Dem letzten Leide
Entgegen trieb mich weißer Sonnen Wut.
Und ich zerbrach die Tempel der Entsagung.

Ist dies der Tod? Sprich, müde Pracht.
Oder werde ich aus Deinen Schächten
Zu lichten nie gekannten Städten steigen
Und jedem Tage seine Donner zeigen?

The weary night glowed from blue wounds
And all the streets lay bare without shame
And all flags screamed into the winds:
And so the day goes to its end.

Once day was so radiant that I spurned the oath
Of contrition and the fixated fervor of angels. Too sweet
Was this agony. Driven to ultimate sorrow, I am loath
To succumb to the raging sun's white heat.
And so I smashed the temple of self-denial.

Is this death? Speak, weary splendor,
Or out of mineshafts I'll rise up from under
To luminous cities yet to be known
And show each day its thunder.

Gewaffnete ziehen die Straßen entlang
Lachende Knaben verführt ihr Gesang
Und durch die Gewirre der Tiere und Plagen
Und Leute und Schreie und gleitenden Wagen
Schneiden die Reihen mit tönendem Gang.

Armed troops march along the streets, their song
Seduces the laughing teen-aged upstarts
And through a jumble of plagues and animal throng
And people and screams and gliding carts
Their ranks cut, with boots resounding so strong.

Tortur

Im Himmel liegen Schwerter wo verborgen.
Ja, wenn ich nur so lange Finger hätte!
So aber hängt man mich an eine Kette,
Hoch in die Luft, so zwischen heut und morgen.

Wer aber band mich fest? Ich möcht es gerne wissen.
Als Wachsfigur beschweb ich diese Stadt.
Man hüllt mich ein in sanften Finsternissen,
Weil sonst die Polizei ein Einsehn hat.

Torture

Swords lie hidden somewhere in the sky.
If only my fingers could sneak that high!
Instead, I'm strung up on a chain and hang in the air
Somewhere between today and tomorrow.

But who bound me so tight? That I'd like to know.
I'm a wax figure hovering over this city,
Enveloped in a soft and darkened lair,
Lest the police come around and see.

Am Lietzensee

Meinem Freunde Georg Heym

Die rote Sandsteinbrücke packt
Staubig die andere Seite vom schwärzlichen Tümpel.
Laternen. Das verirrte Mondlicht zackt
Über Sträucher und Wellen und träges Gerümpel.

Doch zu uns tönt der Abendschrei der Stadt.
Ich spüre noch die Lust der vielen Straßen
Und Trommelwirbel um Fortunas Rad.
Doch du stehst vor mir schläfrig und verblasen.

Feindselig reichst du mir die plumpe Hand,
Von neuem Zorn die starke Stirn betört.
Und als ich längst schon meinen Weg gerannt
Hat alle Schritte noch dein Traum gestört.

Berlin Lietzensee

for my friend Georg Heym

The sandstone bridge, red and dusty, snatches
The other side of the swart puddle.
Lanterns. Wayward moonlight cross-hatches
Shrubs and waves and dull rubble.

Yet resounding out to us: the city's evening peal.
I still feel the thrill of street after street
And the drum-roll 'round Fortuna's Wheel.
Yet you stand before me drowsy and bleak.

Enmity reaching out to me: your clumsy hand.
A new-born rage has your firm forehead beguiled.
And long after off on my way I ran
Your dream still troubled my every stride.

Hundert starke Arme langen
Aus dem Sumpfe nach dir hin.
Donner brummen. Goldne Schlangen
Packen dich an Brust und Kinn.

Und sieh, ein Greis mit weißen Flammenhaaren
Schreit dich pathetisch dabei an:
»Du sollst nun mal zur Hölle fahren!
Da, sieh dir deine Wunder an!

Sind es nicht Farben, die in Fieberjahren
Dein traumbetörtes Auge sich ersehnt?
Bewundre Blitze, die ins Fleisch dir fahren!
Belausch den Tod, der schon im Hirn dir dröhnt!«

Und wütend läufst du immer weiter,
Das Ganze ist zwar zaubertoll,
Doch ist es weiter gar nicht heiter,
Wenn man am Wunder sterben soll.

A hundred strong arms rise
From the swamp and out they reach,
Struggling and straining to draw you in.
Thunder rumbles. Two golden serpents, each
Wrapping 'round your chest and chin.

Look, an aged man with white hair ablaze
Is passionately screaming at you:
"To hell with you! One of these days
Your wonders will be due for review.

Your feverish, dream-duped eye craves
Color. Pay no heed to the agonizing pain,
Marvel at thunderbolts piercing your flesh, eaves-
Drop on death already droning in your brain!"

And on and on you run, eyes all spiteful.
It's all so crazily magical,
But it's not at all delightful
If one dies of a miracle.

Mich treibt mein Tag zum blutigen und harten
Verräter-Werk … Ich weiß, daß Rächer harren
Geschlossenen Helmes. – Ungefügen starren
Zermalmer-Schrittes schreit ich durch die Gärten

My day urges me on to carry out the hard and
Bloody work of a traitor… I know that avengers await,
Their visors down. – The boorish thugs gaze straight
At my crunching strides through the garden

Gebet

Der du den Raum heraufwarfst und das Meer
Und Sonnen, Städte, Wolkenungetüme
Und Engel wacher Nächte –
Du machst die allerhellsten Tage grau
Wie Morgen wilder Städte. Angstgeschrei
Führst du mir her wie zornige Musik. –
Verberge dich, so oft ich feige bin
Vor meiner Schmach im alten Blut der Nacht.

Prayer

You who hurled space and the waters on high
And the sun, cities, billowing cloud colossi,
And angels of wide-awake nights –
You make the brightest days dingy and gray
Like the morning of savage cities. You send
Cries of fear to me like angry music. –
Whenever I'm cowardly, hide from my dishonor
In the ancient blood of the night.

Wie an unsichtbaren Fäden
Rennt er immer hin und her.
Gestern wollte er noch reden,
Heute weiß er es nicht mehr.

»Ist es Irrsinn, ist's Erleben,
Daß man so ins Leere rennt?
Darf man wie 'ne Sonne schweben
Brennend hoch am Firmament?«

As if on invisible wires:
To and fro his constant run.
Once speaking topped his desires.
Today what's done is done.

"Is it nonsense, is it wise,
To run to nowhere and to no one?
May one float like the sun
Burning on high in the skies?"

Lyrischer Abend

. . . . . Wo ein paar weiße Bogenlampen schwanken.
Aus Spiegeln prallen sie mit Fieberblick.
Und ein paar häßliche Gedanken
Packen mich klappernd am Genick.

Die Erde, die am Tag in Flammen dröhnte,
Ist fern und leer.
Nur schnelles Wagenrasseln
Tönt von Straßen her.

Die Nacht ist teufelsrot.
Auf schmalen Wegen
Ein grauer Tod
Kommt uns entgegen.

Lyrical Evening

. . . . . Where a pair of white arc lamps sway in the breeze.
Light bouncing from mirrors with a feverish look.
And a couple of ugly thoughts seize
Me, rattling, by the scruff of my neck.

The earth, that by day roared in flames,
Is now vacant and remote.
Only the rushing clatter of a carriage
Reaches us from the street.

Devilishly red is the night.
On a narrow pathway
A pale ashen gray
Death comes into sight.

Nachtgesang

Das Abendroß zerriß die blauen Himmel.
Blut fiel aufs Meer. Und Fieber flammten auf.
Die Lampen stachen durch die junge Nacht.
Auf Straßen und in weißen Zimmern hell.

Und Menschen winden sich vom Lichte wund.
Die Strolche schreien. Kleine Kinder schluchzen,
Von Wäldern träumend, ängstlich. Ein Verrückter
Hockt lauernd auf im Bette: Soll ich fliehen?

»Was sind wir aus dem Mutterleib gekrochen
Denn jeder möchte doch ein andrer sein.
Und jeder bohrt dir seine Augen ein
Und drängt sich schamlos ein in deinen Traum
Und seine Glieder sind an deinen Knochen
Als gäb es keinen Raum.

Und Menschen wollen immer noch nicht sterben
Und keiner wallt so einsam wie der Mond.
Und selbst der Mond bedeutet nur Verderben.
Denn seine Liebe wird mit Tod belohnt. –

Tief unter mir erstirbt die kranke Nacht.
Und grauenhaft steigt bald der Morgen auf.
Flugs schlägt er tot das Schwarz.
Was tut er wilder
Als Bruder Gestern, den die Nacht verschlang?«

Trompetenstöße vom verfluchten Berge –
Wann sinken Land und Meer in Gott?

Night Song

The evening steed shredded the blue sky.
Blood fell onto the sea. And fever blazed on high.
The lamps pierced the young night.
On streets and in white rooms bright.

And humans writhe, wounded by light.
Idle vagabonds scream. Small children sob,
Anxiously dreaming of forests. A lunatic
Crouches in bed, ears pricked up. Should I flee?

"Why have we crawled from our mother's womb,
For each of us would like to be another.
And everyone bores into you with piercing eye
And bursts shamelessly into your dream.
Limbs pressed against your bones make it seem
As if there were no more room.

And humans still don't want to die.
And no one surges as lonesome as the moon.
And even the moon means nothing but ruin,
For his love is rewarded with a tomb. –

Deep under me, the feeble night dies away
And soon the ghastly morning ascends.
In a flash, it strikes the blackness dead.
What does it do more rashly
Than Brother Yesterday, whom the night consumed?"

A flourish of trumpets from the accursed mountaintop –
When will land and sea sink into godhead?

Stationen eines Dichterlebens

Irene Stratenwerth

„Jakob van Hoddis? Das war mein Onkel", sagte eine Stimme am Telefon von sehr weit weg. Mit diesem Gespräch im Frühjahr 1999 zwischen einer über Achtzigjährigen in einem Kibbuz an der jordanischen Grenze und einer Journalistin in Hamburg begann die vorläufig letzte Wiederentdeckung eines expressionistischen Dichters und seiner verstörenden Lebensgeschichte.

Jakob van Hoddis kam 1887 als Hans Davidsohn zur Welt. Nur für wenige Jahre seines Lebens war er ein produktiver und anerkannter Großstadtdichter. Als er 1942 der Schoa zum Opfer fiel galt er bereits seit Jahrzehnten als unheilbar geisteskrank. Erst nach dem Zweiten Weltkrieg wurde sein schmales Werk wieder entdeckt: 1958 erschien eine erste Werkausgabe im Arche Verlag; in den Sechziger und Siebziger Jahren begeisterte es prominente Dichterkollegen wie Robert Gernhardt, Peter Rühmkorf und Wolf Biermann; 1986 leuchtete eine Biographie von Helmuth Hornbogen seinen Lebensweg aus und noch einmal zehn Jahre widmete sich eine Erzählung von Fritz Bremer dem Schicksal des Dichters und Psychiatriepatienten. Seine Nichten und Neffen, die im Mai 1933 als Halbwüchsige aus Deutschland nach Palästina flohen und später zu Erben der Rechte an seinem Werk wurden, erfuhren davon Jahrzehnte lang nichts. Bis zu jenem Telefongespräch im Mai 1999, dem wenig später eine Reise nach Israel folgte und 2001 eine viel beachtete

Ausstellung in den historischen Räumen der *Stiftung Neue Synagoge Berlin – Centrum Judaicum* und ein Begleitband: *All meine Pfade rangen mit der Nacht. Jakob van Hoddis/Hans Davidsohn (1887–1942).*
So viel Aufmerksamkeit hätte den Dichter wahrscheinlich sehr überrascht und gefreut, denn Erfolg war ihm zu Lebzeiten nur wenig beschieden. Am 16. Mai 1887 wurde er als ältester Sohn des jüdischen Arztes Hermann Davidsohn und seiner Frau Doris, geborene Kempner, in Berlin geboren, ein zunächst zartes, später schwieriges Kind. Ein Zwillingsbruder mit kräftigerer Konstitution kam tot zur Welt. Hans Davidsohn aber blieb kleinwüchsig, wurde nie größer als 1,53 Meter. Wegen seiner angeblich leicht asiatischen Gesichtszüge verspotteten ihn seine Mitschüler als „Chinesen“ und wegen seiner Größe als „Krümel“. Schon im Grundschulalter fiel er durch heftige Wutanfälle auf.
Auf einem Foto aus dem Jahre 1895 posiert der Achtjährige mürrisch, in soldatischer Haltung und mit einer Pickelhaube auf dem Kopf vor einem Gasthof im Harz. Dass seine drei Jahre jüngere Schwester Anna anderthalb Treppenstufen unter ihm steht, soll wahrscheinlich den mangelnden Größenunterschied zwischen den Kindern kaschieren.
Ihre Eltern hängen ganz unterschiedlichen Weltanschauungen an: Der Vater ist Atheist, streng wissenschaftsgläubig und materialistisch. Die Mutter schwärmt idealistisch für deutsche Dichter und ganz besonders für Goethe. Trotz aller Konflikte, die sich in stundenlangen Debatten am Essenstisch der Familie entladen, bemühen sich beide bedingungslos um Zugehörigkeit zur bürgerlichen

Mittelschicht in der wachsenden Großstadt. Die Familie zieht von Friedrichshain nach Kreuzberg und später nach Schöneberg, die fünf Kinder werden in nationalistisch geprägte Schulen wie das Friedrich-Wilhelm-Gymnasium geschickt.

Ihr Ältester eckt dort bald an. „Niemand versteht mich", notiert er als Fünfzehnjähriger, legt sich mit seinen Lehrern an, geht mit achtzehn endgültig von der Schule ab. Ob es bei diesem Entschluss eine Rolle spielte, dass der Schuldirektor Richard Noetel ein enger Freund des berüchtigten Hofpredigers Adolf Stoecker und offener Antisemit war, ist nicht überliefert.

Sein Abitur macht Hans Davidsohn als Externer. Er immatrikuliert sich an der Universität, wird sein Studium aber nie abschließen: Schon früh sind ihm seine Freunde, sind ihm leidenschaftliche Debatten in wissenschaftlich-literarischen Zirkeln wichtiger als akademische Pflichten.

Das Deutschland, in dem er heranwächst, ist zu Beginn des 20. Jahrhundert durch klirrenden Militarismus und erstarrte Herrschaftsstrukturen geprägt. Einerseits. Andererseits verändern rasante Industrialisierung und ebenso schnelle technische Umwälzungen die Gesellschaft spürbar. Nichts passt mehr zusammen. Die Stimmung unter den jungen Männern, die 1907 die *Freie Wissenschaftlichen Vereinigung* gründen und 1909 den *Neuen Club*, ist zum Zerreißen gespannt. Ihr Aufbruch richtet sich gegen alles Überkommene, Verstaubte, „Kommisshafte", aber ein gemeinsames politisches Programm haben sie nicht. Vor allem und in erster Linie sind sie: dagegen.

„Noch nie zuvor hat sich ein ‚Kollektiv' mit so unermüdlichem heiter-verbissenen Ernst durch die einschläfernden Nebelschwaden ihrer gegenwärtigen Geschichtssituation durchgearbeitet", so erinnert sich später Erwin Löwenson an die Anfänge des *Neuen Clubs.* Hans Davidsohn, den er schon aus seiner Schulzeit kennt, bleibt unter diesen Freigeistern ein Fremdling und gilt zugleich als der Begabteste von ihnen.

Ende des Jahres 1909 beginnt er sich Jakob van Hoddis zu nennen: Das Pseudonym formt er aus den Buchstaben seines Nachnamens. Auf Vortragsabenden, die der *Neue Club* in Ateliers und Kaffeehäusern ausrichtet – dem so genannten *Neopathetischen Cabaret* – trägt er erste eigene Gedichte vor.

Fast jeden Abend treffen sie sich im „Café Größenwahn" am Kurfürstendamm (das offiziell *Café des Westens* heißt) und reden sich die Köpfe heiß. Um die sechs Gründungsmitglieder des *Neuen Clubs,* zu denen Jakob van Hoddis gehört, scharen sich junge Maler, Dichter und Schauspieler sowie arriviertere Publizisten wie Herwarth Walden und Else Lasker Schüler. Letztere notiert im November 1910 über einen Aufritt von Jakob van Hoddis: „Auf einmal flattert ein Rabe auf, ein schwarzschillernder Kopf blickt finster über die Brüstung des Lesepults. Jakob van? Er spricht seine kurzen Verse trotzig und strotzend, die sind so blank geprägt, man könnte sie ihm stehlen." Ein anderer Stammgast des Café des Westens, der Grafiker und Schriftsteller Edmund Edel, schreibt 1912 über die Stimmung der Berline Bohème: „Hier werden Weltanschauungen täglich aus dem Ärmel geschüttelt, Existenzen vernichtet, neue Helden auf den

Thron gehoben, Kritik geübt an allem, was man nicht selbst geschaffen hat. Hier wird das große Hohngelächter der Übermenschen angeschlagen."

Jakob van Hoddis erlebt mehr Zerrissenheit als Zugehörigkeit zu diesen Kreisen. Einige seiner Freunde entwickeln sich zu glühenden Kommunisten, doch er überwirft sich mit ihnen. Er selbst sympathisiert zeitweise mit dem Katholizismus, verkündet gar seinen Übertritt zum Christentum, doch offiziell vollzieht er diesen Schritt nie. Seine Waffen gegen die Zumutungen der modernen Welt heißen Hohn, Spott und beißende Ironie. Nur gelegentlich schlägt er zartere Töne an, klingt pathetisch, grüblerisch und hochsensibel. Er will die Dichtkunst neu erfinden und leidet doch so sehr an der Welt, dass er sie kaum noch ertragen kann.

Anfangs werden seine Werke vor allem in Zeitschriften publiziert: Dem *Sturm*, der *Aktion* und dem *Demokrat*. Oft im Ein-Mann-Betrieb produziert verschreiben sich diese Blätter in den Vorkriegsjahren einer neuen, „freiheitlichen" Politik und Kunst. Auch das Gedicht *Weltende* erscheint im Januar 1911 zum ersten Mal im *Demokrat*: Acht Zeilen, die schnell zum „Ohrwurm der zähesten Art" (Robert Gernhardt) werden. Mit einem Schlag ist Jakob van Hoddis allen bekannt, die sich für neuere Kunst und Literatur interessieren.

Doch persönlich geht es bereits bergab mit ihm. Im Februar spaltet sich der *Neue Club* – unter anderem weil van Hoddis hasserfüllt gegen einen Mitbegründer wütet. Im April 1911 stirbt sein Vater. Etwa zur selben Zeit kommt es zum Bruch mit seiner Familie. Im November wird er „wegen Unfleiss" von der Universität exmatrikuliert,

und im Januar 1912 ertrinkt sein enger Freund und Dichterrivale Georg Heym beim Schlittschuhfahren auf der Havel.
Von nun an wirkt Jakob van Hoddis auf seine Freunde zunehmend sprunghaft und unberechenbar, äußert Verfolgungsideen. Sie machen sich Sorgen um ihn und sind doch ratlos. Im Umgang mit dem anderen Geschlecht hat er wenig Glück. Zwei Frauen beschäftigen ihn nachhaltig: Die Schauspielerin und Gelegenheitsprostituierte Emmy Hennings und die Puppenkünstlerin Lotte Pritzel. Beide leben eher in München als in Berlin und beide ziehen Hoddis wohl nie ernsthaft als Liebespartner in Erwägung. Lotte Pritzel widmet er 1914 sein Gedicht *Indianisch Lied*, Emmy Hennings aber hat er schon ein Jahr zuvor geschrieben: „Ich hab dich lieb. Sehr still und wirklich. Das mit Lotte ist man bloß ne Leidenschaft gewesen."
Da hat er seinen ersten Aufenthalt in der Psychiatrie bereits hinter sich. Im September 1912 begibt er sich freiwillig in die Kuranstalt Wolbeck bei Münster, die sich Patienten mit „überreizten Nerven" empfiehlt. Er bleibt dort einen Monat, kehrt dann nach Berlin zurück, wird aber schon Ende Oktober unter Zwang in die psychiatrische Anstalt Nikolassee eingewiesen. Er selbst „wittert Verbindungen", so einer seiner Freunde, sieht sich als Opfer von Machenschaften seiner Familie. Seine Mutter aber schildert ihn als psychisch auffällig, verwahrlost und zeitweise „halb verhungert". Nach sechs Wochen flieht er aus der Klinik, irrlichtert durch Heidelberg, München und Paris und taucht im Frühjahr 1913 wieder in Berlin auf.

Während der *Neue Club* auseinanderbricht, wird der Maler Ludwig Meidner zu seinem engen Freund. Oft besucht er ihn in seinem Atelier in Friedenau. In den Jahren 1913 und 1914 porträtiert Meidner den drei Jahre jüngeren Hoddis zwei Mal. Seine Mappe *Straßen und Cafés* und seine apokalyptischen Landschaftsgemälde wirken wie Illustrationen zu dessen Gedichten.
Der Gegensatz zu einem anderen, engen Malerfreund des Dichters könnte kaum größer sein: Jakob van Hoddis hat Kay Heinrich Nebel als Verlobten seiner Schwester Anna kennengelernt. Erst nachdem diese Verbindung 1911 gelöst wird, intensiviert sich die Freundschaft zwischen den beiden jungen Männern, widmet Hoddis auch ihm ein Gedicht. „Kay", der in den Zwanziger Jahren zu einem führenden Vertreter der neuen Sachlichkeit wird, bleibt eine legendäre Gestalt in der Familiengeschichte: „Jemand deutsches, christliches – Hermann Davidsohn war begeistert" weiß Anna Davidsohns Tochter Chava noch 1999 zu berichten. Der Maler, der nach 1933 zeitweise für den NS-Staat arbeitet, übersteht die Zeit bis 1945 unbehelligt an der Kunstakademie in Kassel, während Ludwig Meidner als „entarteter Künstler" und Jude 1939 nach London fliehen muss.

Seine Verbindung zur realen Welt verliert Jakob van Hoddis wohl schon vor dem Ersten Weltkrieg. Vereinsamt, mit allen zerstritten und im Auftreten sonderbar haust er in einer Atelierwohnung in Halensee, die er mit selbst gemalten christlichen Bilder dekoriert hat. Doris Davidsohn versucht ihrem Sohn eine Einweisung in eine Irrenanstalt zu ersparen, bringt ihn im Herbst 1914 zunächst in einer Kurklinik in Elgersburg/ Thüringen unter und ab Sommer 1915 in „Privatpflege" bei einem Lehrer im nahen Frankenhain. Hoddis scheint seine Existenz als Pflegling klaglos hinzunehmen, fällt im Dorf nur durch sein rastloses Laufen durch die thüringischen Wälder auf. Der Tochter des Lehrers schreibt er 1915, in gestochen scharfer Handschrift, einig nur leicht abgewandelte Zeilen von Jean Paul ins Poesiealbum:

Wirf deinen Anker
Nicht nach der Tiefe
Des Erdenschlammes,
sondern nach der Höhe
des Himmelsblaues
und dein Schifflein
wird glücklich landen
im Sturm.

Dass 1918 ein schmales Heft mit seinen Gedichten unter dem Titel *Weltende* im Verlag der *Aktion* erscheint, dass Kurt Pinthus 1919 seine berühmte, expressionistische Anthologie *Menschheitsdämmerung* mit eben diesem Gedicht eröffnet, nimmt dessen Autor wohl kaum noch zur Kenntnis. Er übersiedelt 1922 von Thüringen nach Tübingen, wird wieder in Privatpflege bei einem Gastwirt untergebracht und noch einmal fünf Jahre später in die Tübinger Universitäts-Nervenklinik eingewiesen. Von dort erfolgt seine Verlegung in die Privatklinik Christophsbad in Göppingen.

Seinen Geschwistern und seiner Mutter entgeht nicht, welches Unheil sich währenddessen gegen sie zusammenbraut: Die Schwestern Anna und Marie verlassen Deutschland am 1. April 1933 – dem Boykotttag gegen die Juden – mit ihren Kindern. Ihre Ehemänner wandern mit ihren Familien noch im Sommer desselben Jahres endgültig in das Britische Mandatsgebiet Palästina aus. Doris Davidsohn, die Mutter, geht mit ihnen.
Aber was wird aus Hans? Welche Gespräche in der Familie über die Zukunft des psychisch kranken Angehörigen geführt wurden, ist nicht bekannt. Hätten sie ihn mitnehmen können? Eine Einreisebewilligung für Palästina wäre dem psychisch kranken 46-Jährigen von der britischen Verwaltung bestimmt nicht erteilt worden.
Doris Davidsohn bringt ihren Sohn schließlich an dem Ort in Deutschland unter, der ihr 1933 noch am sichersten erscheinen muss: Den *Israelitischen Heil- und Pflegeanstalten* in Bendorf-Sayn bei Koblenz. Ihren Bruder bestimmt sie zum Vormund für seinen Neffen. Bereits wenige Monate nach ihrer Ankunft in Tel Aviv stirbt sie dort im Alter von 75 Jahren.
Über das Leben, das Jakob van Hoddis in der Heilanstalt bei Koblenz führte, ist wenig bekannt. Einquartiert in die „ruhige Herrenabteilung" im zweiten Stock einer prachtvollen Jugendstilvilla wird er kaum wahrgenommen haben, was außerhalb des Klinikgeländes vor sich ging. Wahrscheinlich ist er oft und schnell durch den weitläufigen Park der Anstalt gelaufen.
Im Laufe der NS-Jahre entwickelt sich die ehemals noble Kurklinik mehr und mehr zur Zufluchtsstätte

für jüdische Patientinnen und Patienten, Nervenärzte, Krankenschwestern und Pfleger, die in Deutschland nirgendwo sonst noch Platz haben. Die Anstalt wird zur Enklave der Humanität und des jüdischen Lebens, in der die Versorgung mit Lebensmitteln durch eine klinikeigene Landwirtschaft bis zuletzt gesichert ist.
Die angebliche „Gnade“ der Euthanasie bleibt den Patientinnen und Patienten der *Israelitischen Heil- und Pflegeanstalten* erspart. Doch am 30. April 1942 wird Jakob van Hoddis, gemeinsam mit 100 Patientinnen und Patienten und Angehörigen des Pflegepersonals zum Bahnhof von Bendorf-Sayn getrieben und in den Distrikt Lublin deportiert. Wenige Wochen später werden sie alle im Vernichtungslager Sobibor ermordet.
Für seine Familie bleibt sein Schicksal ein Trauma. Die Schuldgefühle, ihn nicht gerettet zu haben, und die Angst vor einer genetischen Belastung kommender Generationen verhindern, dass darüber gesprochen wird. Hinzu kommen der schwierige Existenzkampf in einem fremden, unwirtlichen Land und persönliche Tragödien, Unglücksfälle und Krankheiten.
Doch versteckt haben sich die die Erben des Jakob van Hoddis nie. Auf eine Suchmeldung, die 1999 in einer deutschsprachigen Emigrantenzeitung in Israel veröffentlicht wird, melden sie sich sofort und sind bass erstaunt, dass die Gedichte ihres Onkels und Großonkels in Deutschland inzwischen hochgeschätzt, vielfach publiziert und gelesen werden. Eine seiner Nichten reist 2001 im Alter von 80 Jahren von New York nach Berlin, um an der Eröffnung einer Ausstellung über Jakob van Hoddis in den historischen Räumen der Neuen Synagoge teilzunehmen.

Diesem Interesse und der Aufgeschlossenheit der Erbengemeinschaft des Jakob van Hoddis, die heute in Israel und den USA leben, ist es auch zu verdanken, dass seine Gedichte jetzt erstmals in englischer Übersetzung publiziert werden können.

Alle Zitate nach: Irene Stratenwerth und Stiftung Neue Synagoge Berlin – Centrum Judaicum: *All meine Pfade rangen mit der Nacht. Jakob van Hoddis/Hans Davidsohn (1887–1942).* Frankfurt und Basel 2001

A Poet's Life

Irene Stratenwerth / Maria Lanman (Translation)

"Jakob van Hoddis? He was my uncle," says the voice from very far away on the other end of the line. This conversation between an eighty-year-old woman in a kibbutz on the Jordanian border and a journalist in Hamburg took place in the spring of 1999. It was the start of the most recent rediscovery of an Expressionist poet and his disturbing biography.

Jakob van Hoddis was born Hans Davidsohn in 1887. He was a productive and acknowledged urban poet for only a brief period of his life. He had been regarded as incurably mentally ill for decades when he became a victim of the Shoah in 1942. His slim oeuvre was not rediscovered until after World War II. In 1958, a first volume was published in the Arche Verlag. In the sixties and seventies, his work inspired prominent literary colleagues, including Robert Gernhardt, Peter Rühmkorf, and Wolf Biermann. In 1986, a biography written by Helmuth Hornbogen shed light on his life; ten years later, a semi-biographical story by Fritz Bremer was devoted to the fate of the poet and psychiatric patient.

His nieces and nephews fled to Palestine from Germany as adolescents in 1933. They later inherited the rights to his oeuvre, but they knew nothing of these books for decades, until the telephone call in May 1999. This was soon followed by a trip to Israel and, in Berlin, a highly regarded exhibition in the historic rooms of the *Stiftung Neue Synagoge Berlin – Centrum Judaicum* and an accompanying volume: *All meine Pfade rangen mit der Nacht. Jakob van Hoddis/Hans Davidsohn (1887–1942).*

It is quite likely that the writer would have been amazed and delighted by this attention, as he was only modestly successful during his lifetime. Born in Berlin on May 16, 1887, he was the eldest son of the Jewish physician, Hermann Davidsohn, and his wife, Doris, née Kempner. He was a frail and later difficult child. A larger twin brother died at birth. Hans Davidsohn remained small; he never grew taller than 1.53 meters. His classmates taunted him because of his alleged Asian facial traits and his height, calling him "Chinese" and "crumb-snatcher". As an elementary schoolchild, he was already prone to fits of rage. In a picture taken in 1895, in front of a tavern in the Harz Mountains, the eight-year-old poses sullen-faced in a soldierly posture with a spiked helmet on his head. Placing his three-years-younger sister Anna one and a half steps beneath him is probably meant to conceal the fact that the children are almost the same height.

Their parents have very disparate worldviews. The father is an atheist, with a strong belief in science and materialism. The mother is idealistically inspired by German poets, and Goethe in particular. Despite the conflicts that erupt in hours of debates at the family's dinner table, both parents strive to belong to the bourgeois middle class of the expanding city. The family moves from Friedrichshain district to Kreuzberg, and later to Schöneberg; their five children are sent to schools

with marked nationalistic values, such as the Friedrich-Wilhelm-Gymnasium.
Their eldest child soon shows signs of concerning behavior. At the age of fifteen he notes, "Nobody understands me." He gets into fights with his teachers and finally leaves school at the age of eighteen. It is not known whether this decision was prompted by the fact that the school's director, Richard Noetel, was a close friend of the infamous and openly anti-Semitic court chaplain, Adolf Stoecker.
Hans Davidsohn takes his Abitur examination as an outside student. He enrolls in the university but never graduates. His friends and the passionate debates in scientific-literary circles are soon more important than academic assignments.
At the beginning of the 20th century, clanking militarism and rigid power structures have shaped the Germany he grows up in. On the one hand. On the other hand, the breakneck speed of industrialization and equally swift technical upheavals have significantly altered society. Nothing fits together anymore. The mood among the young men who, in 1907, establish the *Freie Wissenschaftlichen Vereinigung* and, in 1909, the *Neue Club* is strained to the breaking point. Their awakening is directed against entrenched, stale, "soldiery" structures, but they do not have a shared political program. First and foremost they are opposed to everything.
Erwin Löwenson later recalled the beginnings of the *Neue Club* and remarked, "A collective had never worked its way through the sleep-inducing fog patches of its

present historical position with such relentlessly buoyant earnestness." Hans Davidsohn, whom Löwenson knew from his school days, remains a stranger among these freethinkers, yet he is soon regarded as the most talented among them.

By the end of 1909, he starts to call himself Jakob van Hoddis. The pseudonym is formed from the letters in his last name. He recites his first poems at lecture evenings organized by the *Neue Club* in ateliers and cafés – the so-called *Neopathetische Cabaret.*

They meet nearly every evening in "Café Größenwahn" ("Café Megalomania", officially named *Café des Westens*) on Kurfürstendamm and argue hotly. The six founding members of the *Neue Club*, which also include Jakob van Hoddis, are surrounded by young painters, poets, actors, and successful publicists like Herwarth Walden and Else Lasker-Schüler. In November 1910, the latter commented on an appearance by Jakob van Hoddis: "Suddenly a raven fluttered onto the stage, a bright black head scowled over the railing of the lectern. Jakob van? He speaks his short verses with defiance and rage; they have such a radiant sheen that one could steal them from him." In 1912, a regular guest at the *Café des Westens*, the graphic artist and writer Edmund Edel, describes the mood of the Berlin bohemians, "Every day world visions are being produced here just like that, existences destroyed, new heroes lifted to the throne, criticism is dealt out to everything one has not created oneself. This is where the great scornful laughter of the superhumans commences."

Jakob van Hoddis is torn between inner conflict and belonging to these circles. Some of his friends become fervent communists, but he falls out with them. At times, he has Catholic sympathies, and even announces his conversion to Christianity, but he never actually takes this step. His weapons against the unreasonable demands of the modern world are scorn, ridicule, and scathing irony. He occasionally strikes a more delicate key, sounds solemn, brooding, and highly sensitive. He wants to reinvent the art of poetry, and yet he suffers so much from the world that he can hardly bear it anymore.

His works are initially published in magazines: *Sturm*, *Aktion*, and *Demokrat*. Often produced in one-man operations, these pre-war sheets are committed to new, "liberal" principles in politics and art. The poem *Weltende* first appears in January 1911 in the *Demokrat*: eight lines that soon become "the catchiest of their kind" (Robert Gernhardt). All at once, Jakob van Hoddis is known by everyone interested in new art and literature.

But privately things are already going downhill for him. In February, the *Neue Club* splits – partly because van Hoddis, full of hate, rants against a co-founder. His father dies in April 1911. At about this time he breaks off with his family. In November, he is expelled from the university for "lack of diligence", and in January 1912, his close friend and literary rival, Georg Heym, drowns while skating on the frozen River Havel.

From then on, his friends observe a change in Jakob van Hoddis' behavior. He seems increasingly erratic and unpredictable, and he says he feels threatened. His friends worry about him, yet they are at a loss. He does not have much luck in dealings with the opposite sex. Two women leave a lasting impression on him – the actress and casual prostitute, Emmy Hennings, and the puppet artist, Lotte Pritzel. Both of them spend more time in Munich than in Berlin, and neither of them is ever seriously interested in Hoddis as a lover. In 1914, he dedicates his poem *Indianisch Lied* to Lotte Pritzel; but just a year earlier he writes to Emmy Hennings, stating, "I love you. Very quietly and genuinely. Lotte was only a fleeting passion."

By then he has already had his first stay in a psychiatric clinic. In September 1912, he voluntarily admits himself to the Wolbeck Sanatorium near Münster, a clinic for patients with "overwrought nerves". He stays there for one month, returns to Berlin, but, by the end of October, he is committed to the Nikolassee psychiatric clinic. According to one of his friends, he "senses conspiracies" and sees himself as a victim of a family intrigue. But his mother describes him as mentally conspicuous, unkempt, and at times "half starved". He escapes from the clinic after six weeks, wanders through Heidelberg, Munich, and Paris, and reappears in Berlin in the spring of 1913.

While the *Neue Club* falls apart, he becomes close friends with the painter, Ludwig Meidner. Hoddis often visits him in his atelier in Friedenau. In 1913 and 1914, Meidner portrays Hoddis, who is three years his junior. Meidner's portfolio *Straßen und Cafés* (streets and cafés) and his apocalyptic landscape paintings reflect the content of Hoddis' poems.

The contrast to another painter, who is also a close friend of the poet, could not be greater: Jakob van Hoddis met Kay Heinrich Nebel as his sister Anna's fiancé. The friendship between the two young men intensifies after this engagement is broken in 1911, and Hoddis dedicates a poem to him. "Kay", who became a leading representative of the New Objectivity in the twenties, remains a legendary figure in the history of the family. In 1999, Anna Davidsohn's daughter, Chava, still relates, "He was German, Christian – Hermann Davidsohn was delighted." This painter, who occasionally works for the National Socialist state after 1933, survives Nazi rule unscathed at the Kunstakademie in Kassel, whereas Ludwig Meidner, a "degenerate artist" and a Jew, is forced to flee to London in 1939.

It seems as though Jakob van Hoddis loses his connection to the real world before World War I. Lonely, on bad terms with everyone, and behaving oddly, he lives in an attic flat in Halensee district, which he decorates with Christian art he has painted himself. Doris Davidsohn tries to spare her son from being committed to a mental asylum and initially brings him to a sanatorium in Elgersburg, Thuringia in the autumn of 1914. In the summer of 1915, he is put in the "private care" of a teacher in nearby Frankenhain. Hoddis appears to accept his existence as a ward without complaint; only his restless walks in the Thuringian forest make him conspicuous in the village. In 1915, in a neat and clear script, he writes a slightly adapted version of a verse penned by Jean Paul in the friendship book of the teacher's daughter.

Do not throw your anchor
into the depths of the mire,
aim for the skies
and your ship will alight
safely in the storm.

It is unlikely that the author was aware of the slim book of poems titled *Weltende* published by *Aktion* in 1918, or that Kurt Pinthus begins his famous Expressionist anthology *Menschheitsdämmerung* with this very poem. He moves from Thuringia to Tübingen in 1922, is yet again put in the private care of a tavern keeper, and is committed to the University Psychiatric Hospital in Tübingen five years later. From there he is moved to the private Christophsbad clinic in Göppingen.

In the meantime, his siblings and his mother are aware of the disaster looming over them. Together with their children, the sisters Anna and Marie leave Germany on April 1, 1933 – the day that begins the boycott against the Jews. Their husbands immigrate together with their families to the British Mandate of Palestine that summer. Doris Davidsohn, the mother, goes with them.

But what about Hans? It is not known what discussions the family held regarding the future of their mentally ill relative. Would they have been able to take him along? The chances are that British authorities would not have issued the 46-year-old mentally disturbed Hoddis an entry permit for Palestine.

Doris Davidsohn finally moves her son to the one place in Germany, which, in 1933, must seem to present the safest option: The *Israelitischen Heil-und Pflegeanstalten* in Bendorf-Sayn near Koblenz. She appoints her brother as guardian of his nephew. Soon after arriving in Tel Aviv, Doris Davidsohn dies aged 75.

Little is known about Jakob van Hoddis' life in the sanatorium in Koblenz. Living in the "quiet men's section" on the second floor of a magnificent art nouveau villa, it is unlikely that he realized what was going on outside the walls of the clinic. He presumably took frequent, quick walks on the spacious grounds of the clinic.

In the course of National Socialist rule, the previously elegant clinic increasingly becomes a sanctuary for Jewish patients, neurologists, nurses, and caregivers who have nowhere else to go in Germany. The clinic becomes an enclave of humanity and Jewish life, where the food supply is secured – until the end – by the clinic's own farm.

The patients in the *Israelitischen Heil-und Pflegeanstalten* are initially spared the so-called "mercy" of euthanasia. But, on April 30, 1942, together with 100 patients and next of kin of the caregivers, Jakob van Hoddis is taken to the train station in Bendorf-Sayn. From there, they are deported to Lublin district in Poland. A few weeks later, they are murdered in Sobibor death camp.

His fate remains traumatic for his family. Feelings of guilt because they did not rescue him, as well as the fear of a genetic burden for future generations, prevent them from talking about it. Matters are further complicated by the difficult struggle for survival in a foreign, inhospitable country, as well as personal tragedies, accidents, and illnesses.

But Jakob van Hoddis's heirs never disown him. They immediately respond to a missing person announcement that appears in a German language emigrant newspaper in 1999 and are utterly amazed that the poems written by their uncle and great-uncle are now highly esteemed and widely published and read. One of his nieces, aged 80, travels from New York in 2001 to take part in the opening of an exhibition about Jakob van Hoddis in the historic rooms of the Neue Synagoge in Berlin.

This interest and the openness of the community of Jakob van Hoddis heirs who now live in Israel and the United States have made the publication of the English translation of his poems possible.

All quotes from: Irene Stratenwerth/Stiftung Neue Synagoge Berlin – Centrum Judaicum: *All meine Pfade rangen mit der Nacht. Jakob van Hoddis/Hans Davidsohn (1887–1942).* Frankfurt and Basel 2001

Zeittafel

1887
Am 16. Mai kommt Hans Davidsohn in Berlin zur Welt.

1888 – 1894
Seine Geschwister Maria, Anna, Ludwig und Ernst werden geboren.

1897
Die Familie zieht von Friedrichshain nach Kreuzberg und 1901 nach Schöneberg (alles Berlin).

1899 – 1905
Hans Davidsohn besucht das Friedrich-Wilhelm Gymnasium, Berlin.

1906
Immatrikulation als Student der Architektur, 1908 Wechsel zum Fach Alt-Philologie

1909
Der *Neue Club* wird gegründet: Erster öffentlicher Vortrag von Gedichten von Hans Davidsohn.

1910
Das Pseudonym Jakob van Hoddis wird erstmals verwendet.

1911
Erstmalig werden Hoddis-Gedichte in verschiedenen Zeitschriften (*Demokrat*, *Sturm*, *Aktion*) publiziert.

1912
Ende Oktober wird Hans Davidsohn per Zwang in die Heilanstalt *Waldhaus Nikolassee* eingewiesen; am 7. Dezember flieht er von dort.

1913
Aufenthalte in Paris, München und Heidelberg.

1914
Beginn des Ersten Weltkrieges; Van Hoddis wird in einer Privatklinik in Elgersburg/Thüringen untergebracht.

1915 – 1922
Häusliche Pflege beim Rektor Emil Siegling in Frankenhain/Thüringen.

1918
Die Gedichtsammlung *Weltende* erscheint im Verlag der *Aktion*.

1922
Übersiedlung nach Tübingen zum Gastwirt Julius Dieterle.

1927
Einweisung in die Universitäts-Nervenklinik in Tübingen; von dort wird er in die Privatklinik *Christophsbad* in Göppingen verlegt.

1933
Machtergreifung der Nationalsozialisten; Hans Davidsohn wird in den *Israelitischen Heilanstalten* (Bendorf-Sayn) untergebracht, seine Schwestern emigrieren mit ihren Familien nach Palästina.

1942
Am 30. April wird Hans Davidsohn mit 100 weiteren Menschen aus Bendorf-Sayn deportiert, in den Distrikt Lublin verschleppt und dort wenig später ermordet.

Timeline

1887
Hans Davidsohn is born in Berlin on May 16.

1888 – 1894
The births of his siblings, Maria, Anna, Ludwig, and Ernst

1897
The family moves from Berlin Friedrichshain to Kreuzberg district and, in 1901, to Berlin Schöneberg.

1899 – 1905
Hans Davidsohn attends the Friedrich-Wilhelm Gymnasium in Berlin.

1906
Enrollment as a student in architecture; transfers to classical philology in 1908.

1909
The *Neue Club* is founded: first public reading of poems written by Hans Davidsohn.

1910
Adopts the pseudonym Jakob van Hoddis.

1911
Poems by van Hoddis are published for the first time in various magazines (*Demokrat*, *Sturm*, *Aktion*).

1912
Hans Davidsohn is committed to the psychiatric clinic *Waldhaus Nikolassee*; he escapes from the clinic on December 7.

1913
Stays in Paris, Munich, and Heidelberg

1914
World War One erupts. Hans Davidsohn is brought to a private sanatorium in Elgersburg in Thuringia.

1915 – 1922
He is put in the private care of the teacher, Emil Siegling, in Frankenhain in Thuringia

1918
Aktion publishes the collection of poems, *Weltende.*

1922
Moves to Tübingen, where he is put in the care of the tavern-keeper, Julius Dieterle.

1927
Van Hoddis is committed to University Psychiatric Hospital in Tübingen; from there he is moved to the private *Christophsbad* clinic in Göppingen.

1933
The Nazi seizure of power. Hans Davidsohn is brought to the *Israelitischen Heilanstalten* (Bendorf-Sayn); his sisters emigrate together with their families to Palestine.

1942
Together with a group of one hundred people, Jakob van Hoddis is deported from Bendorf-Sayn and taken to the Lublin district in Poland, where they are murdered shortly after.

Literatur

Werkausgaben:
Jakob van Hoddis: *Weltende.* Berlin 1918
Jakob van Hoddis: *Gesammelte Dichtungen.* Hg. Von Paul Pörtner. Zürich 1958
Jakob van Hoddis: *Dichtungen und Briefe.* Herausgegeben von Regina Nörtemann. Zürich 1987
Jakob van Hoddis: *Weltende. Gedichte.* Die zu Lebzeiten veröffentlichten Gedichte. Zürich 2001
Jakob van Hoddis: *Dichtungen und Briefe.* Herausgegeben und kommentiert von Regina Nörtemann, Göttingen 2007

Zu Leben und Werk (Auswahl):
Irene Stratenwerth/Stiftung Neue Synagoge Berlin – Centrum Judaicum: *All meine Pfade rangen mit der Nacht. Jakob van Hoddis/Hans Davidsohn (1887–1942).* Frankfurt und Basel 2001

Fritz Bremer: *In allen Lüften hallt es wie Geschrei. Jakob van Hoddis – Fragmente einer Biographie.* Bonn 1996 und Neumünster 2001

Helmut Hornbogen: *Jakob van Hoddis. Die Odyssee eines Verschollenen.* München 1986 und 2001

Wulf Kirsten: *Wandern über dem Abgrund. Jakob van Hoddis nachgegangen.* Jena 1999

Die Mitwirkenden

Mitch Cohen kam 1952 in Pasadena/Kalifornien zur Welt. Studium an der University of California in Santa Barbara und an der Freien Universität Berlin, wo er seit 1977 lebt. Als Übersetzer, Herausgeber und Autor publizierte er unter anderem: *Ber!in: contemporary writing in East and West Berlin* (Bandanna Books 1983). Deutschsprachige Lyrik veröffentlichte er im *Mitlesebuch 2* und *Mitlesebuch 121* (1994 und 2013 im Aphaia Verlag). 2018 erschien seine englische Übersetzung des kurdischen Nationalepos *Mem und Zin.* 2019 publizierte er Horst Bredekamps *Galileis denkende Hand* auf englisch.

Gregory Divers, geboren 1950, studierte zunächst in den USA, dann 1980/1981 mit einem Fulbright Stipendium in Berlin. Er erforschte und publizierte *The Image and Influence of America in German Poetry since 1945* (Camden House, 2002). Divers ist Autor und emeritierter Professor für Germanistik der Saint Louis University/USA. Seine Übersetzungen erschienen in *Transference, Natural Bridge, No Man's Land* und anderen Literatur-Magazinen. Zur Zeit arbeitet er an einem Buchmanuskript mit Übersetzungen der Gedichte von Yaak Karsunke.

Maria Lanman lebt als Übersetzerin in Hamburg

Irene Stratenwerth lebt als Journalistin, Ausstellungsmacherin und Autorin von Sachbüchern und Belletristik in Hamburg.

The Contributors

Mitch Cohen, born in Pasadena, California in 1952, studied literature at the University of California, Santa Barbara and the Freie Universität Berlin. A translator, editor of English, and writer in English and German, he has lived in Germany since 1975 and in Berlin since 1977. He edited and translated *Ber!in: contemporary writing in East and West Berlin* (Bandanna Books 1983). He published German poetry in *Mitlesebuch 2* and *Mitlesebuch 121* (1994 and 2013 with Aphaia Verlag). He translated the Kurdish national epic *Mem u Zin* from the German translation, 2018 and translated Horst Bredekamp's *Galileo's Thinking Hand*, 2019.

Gregory Divers, born in 1950, studied first in the USA, then in 1980/1981 in Berlin on a Fulbright Scholarship. Author of *The Image and Influence of America in German Poetry since 1945* (Camden House, 2002), he is an author and emeritus professor of German at Saint Louis University. His translations have appeared in *Transference, Natural Bridge, No Man's Land* and other literary magazines; he is currently working on a book-length manuscript of translations of poems by Yaak Karsunke.

Maria Lanman lives in Hamburg where she works as a freelance translator.

Irene Stratenwerth is a journalist, organizer of exhibitions and an author of fiction and nonfiction books. She lives and works in Hamburg.

Aus dem Programm von PalmArtPress

Peter Wortsman
Stimme und Atem / Out of Breath, Out of Mind
Zweizüngige Erzählunge / Two-Tongued Tales
ISBN: 978-3-96258-034-6
Short Stories, 320 Seiten, Hardcover, Deutsch/Englisch

Matthias Buth
Weiß ist das Leopardenfell des Himmels
ISBN: 978-3-96258-035-3
Lyrik, 160 Seiten, Hardcover, Deutsch

Leopold Federmair
Schönheit und Schmerz
ISBN: 978-3-96258-036-0
Divertimenti, 240 Seiten, Hardcover, Deutsch

Bianca Döring
Im Mangoschatten - Von der Vergänglichkeit
ISBN: 978-3-96258-026-1
Textcollage, 138 Seiten, Hardcover, Deutsch

Gabriele Borgmann
Venus AD
ISBN: 978-3-96258-024-7
Künstler-Roman, 184 Seiten, Hardcover, Deutsch

Horst Hussel
FRANZ.
ISBN: 978-3-96258-000-1
Lyrik/Prosa, 236 Seiten, mit Abb. H. Hussel, Hardcover, Deutsch

Carmen-Francesca Banciu
Lebt Wohl, Ihr Genossen und Geliebten!
ISBN: 978-3-96258-003-2
Roman, 376 Seiten, Hardcover, Deutsch

Markus Ziener
DDR, mon amour
ISBN: 978-3-96258-104-8
Roman, 226 Seiten, Hardcover, Deutsch

Ewa Trafna / Uta Schorlemmer
Zwischenwelten *Detroit, Warschau, Berlin*
ISBN: 978-3-96258-008-7
Kunstband, 120 Seiten mit farb. Abb. Ewa Trafna, Hardcover,
Deutsch/Englisch/Polnisch

John Berger / Liane Birnberg
garden on my cheek
ISBN: 978-3-941524-77-4
Kunst mit Lyrik, 90 Seiten, Klappenbroschur, Englisch

Juan Ramón Jiménez
Tagebuch eines frischvermählten Dichters
ISBN: 978-3-941524-97-2
Lyrik, 274 Seiten, Hardcover, deutsche Übersetzung: Leopold Federmair

Reid Mitchell
Sell Your Bones
ISBN: 978-3-96258-022-3
Lyrik, 104 Seiten, Klappenbroschur, Englisch

Kevin McAleer
Errol Flynn - ***An Epic Life***
ISBN: 978-3-96258-005-6
Lyrik, 400 Seiten, Hardcover, Englisch

Nicanor Parra
Parra Poesie
ISBN: 978-3-941524-78-1
Lyrik Übertragung I. Brökel, mit Abb. Ulrike Ertel, 60 Seiten, Hardcover, Spanisch/Deutsch

Karl Corino
Lebenslinien
ISBN: 978-3-941524-98-9,
Lyrik, ca. 240 Seiten, Hardcover, Deutsch

Michael Lederer
In thc Widdle Wat of Time
ISBN: 978-3-941524-70-5
Lyrik, Shortstories, 150 Seiten, Hardcover, Englisch

Manfred Giesler
Bruder Bruno. Jeder gegen Jeden - Giordano Brunos Candelaio.
ISBN: 978-3-941524-96-5
Zwei Theaterstücke, 240 Seiten, Klappenbroschur, Deutsch

Matéi Visniec
MIGRAAAAANTEN!
oder *Wir sind zu viele auf diesem verdammten Boot*
ISBN: 978-3-96258-002-5
Theaterstück, 200 Seiten, Hardcover, Deutsch/Englisch